全国高等教育商务英语规划系列教材

商务英语应用文写作

A Practical Coursebook for Business English Writing

主　编　孙志祥　朱义华
副主编　孙亚玲　万　佳　方小勇
　　　　毛卫强　王　翔

苏州大学出版社

图书在版编目(CIP)数据

商务英语应用文写作 = A Practical Coursebook for Business English Writing / 孙志祥,朱义华主编. —苏州:苏州大学出版社,2022.3
全国高等教育商务英语规划系列教材
ISBN 978-7-5672-3766-7

Ⅰ. ①商… Ⅱ. ①孙… ②朱… Ⅲ. ①商务-应用文-写作-高等学校-教材 Ⅳ. ①F7

中国版本图书馆 CIP 数据核字(2022)第 005105 号

书　　　名:	商务英语应用文写作
	A Practical Coursebook for Business English Writing
主　　　编:	孙志祥　朱义华
策划编辑:	汤定军
责任编辑:	汤定军
装帧设计:	吴　钰
出版发行:	苏州大学出版社(Soochow University Press)
社　　　址:	苏州市十梓街1号　邮编:215006
印　　　刷:	江苏凤凰数码印务有限公司
邮购热线:	0512-67480030
销售热线:	0512-67481020
开　　　本:	787 mm×1 092 mm　1/16　印张:13.25　字数:315千
版　　　次:	2022年3月第1版
印　　　次:	2022年3月第1次印刷
书　　　号:	ISBN 978-7-5672-3766-7
定　　　价:	48.00元

凡购本社图书发现印装错误,请与本社联系调换。服务热线:0512-67481020
苏州大学出版社网址http://www.sudapress.com
苏州大学出版社邮箱sdcbs@suda.edu.cn

全国高等教育商务英语规划系列教材

顾　问　徐青根　鲁加升

编　委（以姓氏笔画为序）

于延梅	王　娅	王　翔	王红华
王金华	王德丽	毛卫强	文　格
方小勇	朱冬梅	刘　萱	孙亚玲
孙志祥	李卫东	李太志	李甜甜
杨　晓	步阳辉	张　莹	张　涛
张夏菲	陈　羔	陈　培	陈东东
林又佳	李　宇	金焕荣	郑　骏
施　翔	姚春宁	姚菊霞	袁海燕
顾　红	顾　薇	顾秀梅	徐　健
徐　源	董　坤	程进军	曾　艳
潘　珺	穆连涛		

策　划　汤定军

编者的话

　　随着国际化不断深入,社会各界对商务英语人才的需求持续升温。在商务英语教学和培训中,自2007年商务英语本科专业获准设立以来,开设商务英语课程的院校与日俱增,目前对优秀商务英语教材的需求越来越迫切。

　　根据教育部《高等学校英语专业教学大纲》的课程描述,"应用文写作"课程的目的在于使学生了解应用文的特点和掌握应用文的写作能力。通过应用文阅读和应用文写作的训练,学生可以熟悉应用文的语言特点、篇章结构及基本格式,独立撰写或起草各类文件和信函。

　　在《商务英语应用文写作》教材的编写过程中,编者坚持"写作指南＋范文阅读＋写作训练"的应用文写作教学原则。教材内容贴近商务实际,涵盖了各类应用文写作,包括备忘录、通知、请柬、祝酒词、会议纪要、日程安排表、图表、建议书、报告、报道、商业广告、企业介绍、简历和申请函、文凭证书、公共标识语、问卷调查表等。每个单元由相关写作知识、示范阅读、注释、交际园地(练习)等几个部分组成。在练习设计中,编者重视借助案例学习增强读者在英语交际背景下分析和解决问题的能力。

　　本书主要编写人员为孙志祥、王翔、方小勇、孙亚玲、毛卫强、顾红、林又佳、张莹等。本书编者衷心感谢苏州大学出版社领导及汤定军先生的关心和支持,感谢丁锡芬、赵洪娟、周伟、王芳等的热心帮助。

　　由于编者水平有限,书中错误或不妥之处在所难免,敬请读者不吝赐教。

孙志祥
2021年10月
于江南大学

使用说明

　　本书可以作为本专科英语专业、国际经济与贸易专业、涉外文秘专业、汉语国际教育专业及其他涉外专业的应用文写作教材。本教材同时可以作为企业在职人员培训时使用,以及有志于从事国际商务活动的人士自学之用。

　　本教材每单元由相关知识与写作指南、示范阅读、注释和交际园地等部分组成。相关知识和写作指南部分详细介绍了与主题相关的知识和写作原则。示范阅读部分主要选取了具有代表性的范例供读者阅读与赏析,在阅读中体味与把握写作原则和要领。注释部分包括一些常用词汇和表达方式,以及对文中一些要点的补充。交际园地部分包括简答题和案例分析。简答题旨在帮助读者进一步理清写作原则与要领,案例部分则给读者提供分析解决实际问题的机会,提高其写作技能和水平。

　　全书共 16 个单元,用作全日制学生的教材时,建议一周开设 2 个课时,每 2 个或 3 个课时讲解一个单元。此外,由于本书涵盖内容较广,教师可根据自己学校的专业特点和相关课程开设情况酌情选讲,自行安排讲解课时和顺序。

Contents

Unit 1   Memos   1

1.1   The Layout of Memos   1
1.2   The Planning of Memos   3
1.3   The Tone of Memos   4
1.4   Presentation of Content   5
1.5   Effective Memo Checklist   5
1.6   Sample Memos   5
1.7   Notes   9
1.8   Communication Laboratory   9

Unit 2   Notices   13

2.1   Formats of Notices   13
2.2   The Layout of Notices   13
2.3   How to Write a Notice   14
2.4   Sample Notices   15
2.5   Notes   20
2.6   Communication Laboratory   20

Unit 3   Invitations   22

3.1   Categories of Invitations   22
3.2   The Layout of Invitations   22
3.3   Sample Invitations   24
3.4   Notes   30
3.5   Communication Laboratory   30

Unit 4   Toasts   31

4.1   The Layout of Toasts   32

4.2	The Planning of Toasts	35
4.3	The Tone of Toasts	35
4.4	Presentation of Content	36
4.5	Effective Toast Checklist	36
4.6	Sample Toasts	37
4.7	Notes	44
4.8	Communication Laboratory	45

Unit 5 Minutes   48

5.1	The Layout of Meeting Minutes	49
5.2	Do's and Don'ts in Meeting Minutes Writing	49
5.3	Sample Minutes	50
5.4	Notes	52
5.5	Communication Laboratory	53

Unit 6 Itineraries   54

6.1	The Layout of Itineraries	55
6.2	The Planning of Itineraries	58
6.3	The Tone of Itineraries	58
6.4	Presentation of Itineraries	59
6.5	Effective Itinerary Checklist	59
6.6	Sample Itineraries	60
6.7	Notes	66
6.8	Communication Laboratory	68

Unit 7 Forms and Diagrams   69

7.1	Types of Forms	69
7.2	Types of Diagrams	73
7.3	Notes	76
7.4	Communication Laboratory	79

Unit 8 Proposals   81

8.1	Introduction	81
8.2	The Parts of a Proposal	81
8.3	Sample Proposals	87

8.4	Notes	93
8.5	Communication Laboratory	93

Unit 9　Reports　96

9.1	Categories of Reports	96
9.2	Steps of Report Writing	97
9.3	The Layout of Reports	97
9.4	Sample Reports	100
9.5	Notes	108
9.6	Communication Laboratory	109

Unit 10　Articles　110

10.1	The Format of Business Articles	110
10.2	Four-Step Approach for Article Writing	110
10.3	Writing Guide	111
10.4	Sample Articles	114
10.5	Notes	121
10.6	Communication Laboratory	121

Unit 11　Business Advertisements　122

11.1	Categories of Advertisements	122
11.2	Components of Advertisement Copy	123
11.3	English in Advertising	126
11.4	Sample Advertisements	130
11.5	Notes	132
11.6	Communication Laboratory	135

Unit 12　Business Profiles　137

12.1	The Layout of Business Profiles	137
12.2	Sample Business Profiles	142
12.3	Notes	146
12.4	Communication Laboratory	148

Unit 13　Resumes and Letters of Application　　149

13.1　Resumes　　149
13.2　Letters of Application　　156
13.3　Notes　　166
13.4　Communication Laboratory　　168

Unit 14　Certificates and Credentials　　170

14.1　The Layout of Certificates and Credentials　　170
14.2　Sample Certificates and Credentials　　171
14.3　Notes　　176
14.4　Communication Laboratory　　177

Unit 15　Public Signs　　178

15.1　The Layout of Public Signs　　179
15.2　The Planning of Public Signs　　181
15.3　The Tone of Public Signs　　181
15.4　Presentation of Public Signs　　181
15.5　Effective Public Sign Checklist　　182
15.6　Sample Public Signs　　183
15.7　Notes　　184
15.8　Communication Laboratory　　185

Unit 16　Questionnaires　　186

16.1　The Steps Required to Design and Administer a Questionnaire　　186
16.2　Points Considered when Writing and Interpreting Questionnaires　　186
16.3　Sample Questionnaires　　189
16.4　Notes　　195
16.5　Communication Laboratory　　195

References　　199

Memos and letters are the two most common types of business communication. Memos resemble letters in that they communicate information and are commonly used in the world of business writing. Letters are used to communicate with someone outside the organization while memos are an important means by which employees within an organization communicate with each other.

1.1 THE LAYOUT OF MEMOS

Because the memo form was developed to save time, the formality of an inside address, salutation, and complimentary closing is omitted. Most companies have memo stationery with a preprinted heading. Different companies, however, may use different formats and even within a company, different departments may write memos in different formats. Nevertheless, a memo should include the following information:
- Who is the memo **to**?
- Who is the memo **from**?
- What is the **subject** of the memo?
- What is the **date**?

These should be positioned as shown in the following examples.

Format 1

```
                        MEMO
    To
    From
    Subject
    Date
```

Format 2

```
                        MEMO
    To
    From
    Date
                    (Title Informing of Subject)
```

Format 3

```
                        MEMO
    Date:
    To:
    From:
    Subject:
```

Format 4

```
              WORLDWIDE SHIPPING COMPANY
                     Interoffice Memo
    To:                                  From:
    Subject:                             Date:
```

The To and From. In the *To* and *From* sections, the business title of each person is often included, particularly when the memo is being sent to a person whose office is in another city. In the *To* section, a courtesy title—Miss, Mrs., Ms., Mr., Dr. —is often included. However, in the *From* section, the writer's choice of whether to use a courtesy title or not depends upon the degree of formality that he decides to use.

The memo forms used in large companies may also include other details to facilitate communication among co-workers in various departments and branches of the firm.

Format 5

```
              WORLDWIDE SHIPPING COMPANY
                     Interoffice Memo
    Date: July 17, 2021
    Subject: Ordering of company-headed stationery
    To: Mr. Arthur Foley, Office Manager    From: Peter Smith
                                            Organization: Logistics Service
                                            Location: CA 12
                                            Phone: 341-6639
```

The writer's job title, for example, "job manager" may be included. Some firms insist on the job title as house-style. On its own, without a personal name, the job title would be very formal. Added to a name, it gives a slight touch of formality. In order of formality the possibilities are:
- Office Manager (very formal)
- Mr. Smith, office manager (formal)
- Mr. Peter Smith, office manager (rather less formal)
- Mr. Peter Smith (average formality)
- Mr. Peter Smith, office manager (average formality)
- Peter Smith (slightly informal)
- Peter, office manager (informal)
- Peter (very informal)

The Subject and Date. The beginning of a memo is usually the subject line. It is a brief statement telling what the memo is about and helps the reader to prepare for the contents.

The subject line is not a complete sentence but rather a concise phrase that gives the reader the topic plus a focus. Some companies prefer to have the subject line typed in all caps.

One-word subject lines don't communicate effectively, as in the following flawed example.

Subject: Stationery

An improved subject line would read as follows:

Subject: Ordering of Company-Headed Stationery

This subject gives the topic (Company-Headed Stationery) plus a focus (ordering).

Complete dates are just as important on memos as they are on letters. Dates are necessary for future reference to prevent miscommunication.

The Message. Memos solve problems either by informing the reader about new information, like policy changes, price increases, etc., or by persuading the reader to take an action, such as attending a meeting, or changing a current production procedure. Regardless of the specific goal, memos are most effective when they connect the purpose of the writer with the interests and needs of the reader.

1.2 THE PLANNING OF MEMOS

Like business letters, most memos follow a direct organization plan. The steps in organizing a direct plan memo are: identifying and stating the main points, planning the order of supporting points, evidence, or arguments, and finally concluding with suggestions for future action or requesting guidance of future action.

Occasionally, however, you may find it necessary to write a bad-news or persuasive memo. When you communicate bad news, you expect to arouse strong feelings of disappointment. The goal of the bad-news strategy then is to avoid adding anger and ill will to the disappointment your reader will feel. The bad-news strategy can be used when both of the following conditions occur:
- When the message is expected to upset the reader significantly.
- When minimizing bad feelings is worth the extra time and cost.

Most bad-news messages begin with some comments designed to put the reader in a neutral, reasonable, rational frame of mind for the reasoning that follows. The transition from the opening to the reasoning must be graceful, or the reader will realize that you are shifting gears.

One way to organize the reasoning is to begin with specifics and work toward conclusions. Begin by simply stating the key facts your refusal is based on. Then show how they lead to the conclusion that you must refuse the request.

Whereas in the bad-news strategy the goal is to reduce negative emotions, in persuasion the goal is to arouse the kind of positive emotions that will motivate the audience to do what you want.

A persuasive approach to communicate is appropriate when you must get someone to do something that he or she wouldn't do if you merely requested it. To achieve your goal, you must not only provide information but also convince your audience that you are right.

The general plan for a persuasive message is as follows. The beginning sentences secure the reader's interest and present the basic motivational appeal, namely the benefit to the reader. The body justifies in detail your argument that by acting as you request, the reader will in the end get the benefit you are promising. The ending calls for action.

1.3 THE TONE OF MEMOS

When you are writing a memo, you are writing to someone with whom you work every day. The golden rule is to write as you would like to be written to.

Tone refers to the author's voice. The tone of a memo can range from subjective and emotional to objective and balanced. However, in business and technical writing, it is common to write in an objective and low-key tone rather than a dramatic tone. The number of adjectives and adverbs will influence the tone, as will the choice of pronouns. The fewer the adjectives and adverbs, the more objective the tone. In addition, the tone is objective when *I* and *we* are avoided.

The author's tone is a result of word choice and is determined by the purpose and goal of the document. The tone of the memo is influenced by the position held by the author in relation to that held by the receiver. Also, the topic under discussion plays an important role in determining the tone.

1.4 PRESENTATION OF CONTENT

The presentation of your ideas matters; you have to market them. Memos should look as professional as are feasible. It should be formatted so that important ideas can be taken at a glance. Try to make your text more reader-friendly by applying some of the highlighting techniques: fonts, headings, white space, charts, graphs, pictures, bolded words, bullets and graphics. Remember, though, the important consideration is professionalism not creativity.

1.5 EFFECTIVE MEMO CHECKLIST

The following is a list of points to check when you write a memo.
- Have you used the correct memo format, including to, from, date and subject line?
- Will the person who receives the memo be able to understand the message?
- Have you included all relevant information? Is any information missing that will hinder understanding of the message?
- Is your writing style concise? Have you included any irrelevant information?
- Have you written appropriately to your audience? Have you achieved the correct tone? Is the language appropriate for a memo? Is it too polite? Is it too formal or too informal?
- Is your page layout reader-friendly? Have you used highlighting techniques for accessibility?
- Have you checked spelling, grammar and punctuation?

1.6 SAMPLE MEMOS

Sample 1 (1)

MEMO

Date: September 1, 2021
To: Center Interns
From: Center Team Leader
Subject: Standard Format for Memos

In this sample, I have outlined the basic format requirements for a standard memo. You may be familiar with the memo templates that many word processing packages offer—you will notice that there are several variations on the basic format, but the required elements are the same. In any memo, you should include:
- Date;

- Name or position of the people to whom the memo is being sent (if there are multiple recipients, list the names in alphabetical order according to last name; you can also include a "CC" line below the "To" line and list the names of your secondary audience—that is, people who may be interested in the memo but are not directly responsible for responding to it);
- Name or position of the sender (often, the sender will write her/his initials next to her/his name on the memo—this acts as a signal that the sender has verified and approved the memo content);
- Subject line;
- Body text.

The Use of Margins

The margins for a typical memo are a 1.5 inch left margin, 1 inch right margin, and 1 inch margin at the top and bottom of the paper. You can adjust these margins slightly to make your memo fit on one page, or to space the information so that page breaks do not happen at awkward places—for example, when you are at the end of a paragraph and only three or four words flow over to the next page. All paragraphs and headings should be lined up with the left margin.

How to Use Single, Double, and Triple Spacing

Text spacing is an important navigational tool in a memo. Some conventions ask you to double space between the date, to/from, and subject lines and between each paragraph, others use single spacing in the block. Triple space before each heading within the body of the memo. Do not double space the body text of your memo.

Using Headings

If your memo is more than two or three paragraphs, including headings can be helpful for your reader—be sure to use headings that capture the key topic of that section and capitalize each major word of the heading. Bolding or underlining the heading will help the visual design of your memo.

Closing

Provide some conclusion to your memos with an invitation for further discussion or feedback, or with contact information. While you do not use a closing salutation for a memo, as you do with a letter, providing contact information and a conclusion indicates that you are engaging your reader rather than talking at them.

Sample 1 (2)

MEMO

Date: September 1, 2021
To: All Employees
From: James McDonald, President
Subject: Screening for High Blood Pressure

  The company will provide free blood pressure tests for all employees who wish to participate during work hours on September 17 and 18 in the Dining Hall behind the Administration Building.

  Hypertension, or high blood pressure, is a serious condition that increases the risk of heart disease and other illnesses, but it's readily controlled under the care of your own physician. The test is quick and entirely painless.

  This screening is voluntary, and you're under no obligation to be tested. Results will be communicated to you immediately. No record of your test results will be kept by the company.

  Department heads will be scheduling release time for employees who wish to participate.

Sample 1 (3)

MEMO

To: John Erickson, Supervisor
From: Jean James, Director
Date: September 1, 2021
Re: Use of South Parking Lot by Kite Club

  Because we occasionally receive requests like yours to use the south parking lot for club and church activities, last year we checked with our insurance company to determine our liability coverage in such situations. According to our agent, our liability insurance covers only official company use of that property, that is, use directly related to official company activities.

  Since our company values community service such as your present leadership in the Kite Club, we checked to see how much it would cost to extend our insurance to cover community activities on our property. We found the cost prohibitively high. In addition, we considered the possibility of allowing organizations to use the parking lot after signing a waiver of any future claim against our company, but our lawyer indicated that such an arrangement would not adequately protect the company. As a result, we must limit the use of company property only to official company activities.

Sample 1 (4)

MEMO

To: All Executives
From: Randolph Gray, Chief Executive Officer
Subject: Business Conferences via Global Television to Begin in November
Date: July 18, 2021

  For your information, Intercontinental Hotels Corporation (IHC) and Comsat General Corporation have announced an equally owned joint venture to provide international televised conference service available to the public. The service, to begin in November, initially will link IHC's hotels in New York and London. The link will enable small groups, such as business executives, to conference with two-way audio, video, and print-out facilities.

Paul Sheeline, Chief Executive Officer of IHC, said the system would be expanded later to include Houston, Paris, Frankfurt, Riyadh, and Tokyo. He added that the system could be adapted to handle large groups.

Richard Bodman, President of Comsat General, said that prices for use of the system would vary, depending on which facilities a customer wanted to use. But he added that a typical meeting would cost between $1,500 and $2,000 an hour. The system will depend on satellites to beam signals.

As travel costs have increased, the use of televised conferences has grown. "It makes more sense to get half-dozen executives into our hotel in New York for a two-hour teleconference with London, rather than taking the time and going to the expense of flying them all there," Mr. Sheeline said. Because of time differences, officials of Comsat General and IHC said their system would be available around the clock.

Please consider using this system in communicating with your subsidiaries around the world when more than three individuals are involved. The company can save time and travel expenses by having conferences in this mode.

Sample 1 (5)

MEMO

To: All Staff
From: Helen Shakespeare, Office Manager
Subject: Office Paper Recycling Program Kickoff
Date: August 20, 2021

We will be starting an office paper recycling program to recover computer paper, newspaper and paper bags. The program will take only a few minutes of your time each week and will require only minor changes in your work habits. Your participation in this program is necessary for its success.

At the orientation session on August 22, 2021 at 9:15 in the Auditorium, Mr. Jones will explain the details of the program to you and provide you with containers for storing the paper to be recycled. By taking an active part in this program, you will help accomplish our goals of reducing waste and conserving valuable natural resources not only for our department but for our community as well. Waste paper (white ledger and computer paper, colored paper, newspaper, paper bags, paper board, and cardboard packaging) makes up as much as 41 percent of our nation's solid waste. One ton of recovered paper saves over three cubic yards of landfill space. Besides helping conserve landfill space, our program will help conserve natural resources.

You will receive a desktop container for your daily recyclable paper. Once your desktop container is full, please empty it in the centrally located metal white and red intermediate container.

Thank you in advance for your participation in this worthwhile endeavor. If you have questions or would like to assist in the program, call Miss Porter at 878-012.

1.7 NOTES

(1) subject line: one concerning which something is said or done 事由

(2) re: concerning 事由

(3) memo template: a pattern used as a guide in writing a memo 备忘录模板

(4) orientation session: introductory instruction concerning a new situation （任职、上学等之前的）介绍会

(5) shift gears: to make a change 改变方式

1.8 COMMUNICATION LABORATORY

A. Give a brief answer to the following questions.

(1) What are the distinctions between memos and letters?

(2) Why is a subject line in a memo important?

(3) What are the highlighting techniques you can use in a memo?

(4) What is the writing style you should strive for in a memo?

B. Case Study

(1) You work for Wonder International Trading Group. The office manager is Miss Jean James. You arrive at work one morning and find the following note from her on your desk. Carry out her instructions.

> Write a memo under my name to all the company's representatives, informing them that the new supply of company-headed writing paper, and ballpens embossed with the company's name and address, which are to be given to customers, have arrived and will be available to the company reps from next Wednesday from the office. I need to know in writing by next Tuesday the quantities of these items each rep requires.

(2) Read the following web exclusive and discuss the role memos may play.

Double Standards?

A Justice Department memo proposes that the United States hold others accountable for international laws on detainees—but that Washington did not have to follow them itself.

By **Michael Isikoff**
Newsweek
Updated: 11:28 a.m. ET May 25, 2004

In a crucial memo written four months after the September 11, 2001 terror attacks, Justice Department lawyers advised that President George W. Bush and the U.S. military did not have to comply with any international laws in the handling of detainees in the war on terrorism. It was that conclusion, say some critics, that laid the groundwork for aggressive interrogation techniques that led to the abuses at the Abu Ghraib prison in Iraq.

The draft memo, which drew sharp protest from the State Department, argued that the Geneva Conventions on the treatment of prisoners of war did not apply to any Taliban or Al Qaeda fighters being flown to the detention center at Guantanamo Bay, Cuba, because Afghanistan was a "failed state" whose militia did not have any status under international treaties.

But the Jan. 9, 2002 memo, written by Justice lawyers John Yoo and Robert J. Delahunty, went far beyond that conclusion, explicitly arguing that no international laws—including the normally observed laws of war—applied to the United States at all because they did not have any status under federal law.

"As a result, any customary international law of armed conflict in no way binds, as a legal matter, the President or the U.S. Armed Forces concerning the detention or trial of members of Al Qaeda and the Taliban", according to a copy of the memo obtained by NEWSWEEK. A copy of the memo is being posted today on *Newsweek*'s website.

At the same time, and even more striking, according to critics, the memo explicitly proposed a de facto double standard in the war on terror in which the United States would hold others accountable for international laws it said it was not itself obligated to follow.

After concluding that the laws of war did not apply to the conduct of the U.S. military, the memo argued that President Bush could still put Al Qaeda and Taliban fighters on trial as war criminals for violating those same laws. While acknowledging that this may seem "at first glance, counter-intuitive", the memo states this is a product of the president's constitutional authority "to prosecute the war effectively".

The two lawyers who drafted the memo, entitled "Application of Treaties and Laws to Al Qaeda and Taliban Detainees", were key members of the Justice Department's Office of Legal Counsel, a unit that provides legal advice to the White House and other executive-branch agencies. The lead author, John Yoo, a conservative law professor and expert on international law who was at the time deputy assistant attorney general in the office, also crafted a series of related memos—including one putting a highly restrictive interpretation on an international torture convention—that became the legal framework for many of the Bush administration's post-9/11 policies. Yoo also coauthored another OLC memo entitled "Possible Habeas Jurisdiction Over Aliens Held in Guantanamo Bay, Cuba", that concluded that U.S. courts could not review the treatment of prisoners at the base.

Critics say the memos' disregard for the United States' treaty obligations and international law paved the way for the Pentagon to use increasingly aggressive interrogation techniques at Guantanamo Bay—including sleep deprivation, use of forced stress positions and environmental manipulation—that eventually were applied to detainees at the Abu Ghraib prison in Iraq. The customary laws of war, as articulated in multiple international treaties and conventions dating back centuries, also prohibit a wide range of conduct such as attacks on civilians or the murder of captured prisoners.

Kenneth Roth, the executive director of Human Rights Watch, who has examined the memo, described it as a "maliciously ideological or deceptive" document that simply ignored U. S. obligations under multiple international agreements. "You can't pick or choose what laws you're going to follow," said Roth. "These political lawyers set the nation on a course that permitted the abusive interrogation techniques" that have been recently disclosed.

When you read the memo, "the first thing that comes to mind is that this is not a lofty statement of policy on behalf of the United States," said Scott Horton, president of the International League for Human Rights, in an interview scheduled to be aired tonight on PBS's "Now with Bill Moyers" show. "You get the impression very quickly that it is some very clever criminal defense lawyers trying to figure out how to weave and bob around the law and avoid its applications."

At the time it was written, the memo also prompted a strong rebuttal from the State Department's Legal Advisor's office headed by William Howard Taft IV. In its own Jan. 11, 2002, response to the Justice draft, Taft's office warned that any presidential actions that violated international law would "constitute a breach of an international legal obligation of the United States" and "subject the United States to adverse international consequences in political and legal fora and potentially in the domestic courts of foreign countries."

"The United States has long accepted that customary international law imposes binding obligations as a matter of international law," reads the State Department memo, which was also obtained by *Newsweek*. "In domestic as well as international fora, we often invoke customary international law in articulating the rights and obligations of States, including the United States. We frequently appeal to customary international law." The memo then cites numerous examples, ranging from the U. S. Army Field Manual on the Law of Land Warfare ("The unwritten or customary law of war is binding upon all nations," it reads) to U. S. positions in international issues such as the Law of the Sea.

But the memo also singled out the potential problems the Justice Department position would have for the military tribunals that President Bush had recently authorized to try Al Qaeda members and suspected terrorists. Noting that the White House counsel Alberto Gonzales had publicly declared that the persons tried in such commissions would be charged with "offenses against the international laws of war", the State Department argued that the Justice position would undercut the basis for the trials.

"We are concerned that arguments by the United States to the effect that customary international law is not binding will be used by defendants before military commissions (or in proceedings in federal court) to argue that the commissions cannot properly try them for crimes under international law," the State memo reads. "Although we can imagine distinctions that might be offered, our attempts to gain convictions before military commissions may be undermined by arguments which call into question the very corpus of law under which offenses are prosecuted."

The Yoo-Delahunty memo was addressed to William J. Haynes, then general counsel to the Defense Department. But administration officials say it was the primary basis for a Jan. 25, 2002, memo by White House counsel Gonzales—which has also been posted on *Newsweek*'s website—that urged the president to stick to his decision not to apply prisoner-of-war status under the Geneva Conventions to captured Al Qaeda or Taliban fighters. The president's decision not to apply such status to the detainees was announced the following month, but the White House never publicly referred to the Justice conclusion that no international laws—including the usual laws of war—applied to the conflict.

One international legal scholar, Peter Spiro of Hofstra University, said that the conclusions in the memo related to international law "may be defensible" because most international laws are not binding in U.S. courts. But Spiro said that "technical" and "legalistic" argument does not change the effect that the United States still has obligations in international courts and under international treaties. "The United States is still bound by customary international law," he said.

One former official involved in formulating Bush administration policy on the detainees acknowledged that there was a double standard built into the Justice Department position, which the official said was embraced, if not publicly endorsed, by the White House counsel's office. The essence of the argument was, the official said, "it applies to them, but it doesn't apply to us." But the official said this was an eminently defensible position because there were many categories of international law, some of which clearly could not be interpreted to be binding on the president. In any case, the general administration position of not applying any international standards to the treatment of detainees was driven by the paramount needs of preventing another terrorist attack. "The Department of Justice, the Department of Defense and the CIA were all in alignment that we had to have the flexibility to handle the detainees—and yes, interrogate them—in ways that would be effective," the official said.

Unit 2 Notices

Notice, the most commonly used practical writing, notifies the public, inside or outside an organization, of some information: to make known something about to happen or, sometimes, something that has happened.

The information provided by notices is in great varieties: the change of address or telephone number of a company, the setting-up of a new company or a new branch, merger of business, the arrangements of a meeting or of an activity, the appointment of somebody, the implementation of some new regulations, and some warnings. Based on the different kinds of information conveyed, notices can be divided into two categories: the notice giving full message of information and the notice giving a warning or an instruction.

2.1 FORMATS OF NOTICES

There are many ways to send notices. It can be in the format of mail, the format of leaflet, or the format of poster.

Some notices are sent in the format of letter. This type of notice is used when the information is conveyed to a limited number of people. Now with access to the Internet almost everywhere, sending notices by e-mail may be the best choice for its swiftness, convenience, and low cost.

Another format of notice is leaflet, which is often used for business promotion. To this kind of notices is often attached a form, for the reader to fill in and send back to obtain some offers like a discount.

Notices can also be in the format of poster. Written on blackboards or put up on bulletin boards, poster notice is a common means for an organization to inform its staff of some activities such as meetings, holidays or visits.

In this unit, the notices in the format of posters are to be discussed.

2.2 THE LAYOUT OF NOTICES

A notice is usually composed of four components: headline, body, the name and position of the person who writes it, and the date.

A notice requires a clear headline at the top, which can help to catch the reader's eyes. The function of a notice headline is to inform the reader, at his first glance, the subject of the notice. A notice to announce arrangements of a meeting, for example, can be titled "Notice of Meeting", and a notice for something missing usually has the title of "Lost" or "Missing".

The body is the main part of a notice. In this section it is essential that all the necessary information is given so that the reader can understand the information and act on it. A notice of a meeting or a gathering, for example, should state clear the time, the place and some other information of the meeting or gathering. Notices of lectures or talks should also include background information about the speakers.

In most notices the name of the person who writes the notice and the date are placed at the bottom. In some notices the date is found at the right end of the line below the headline.

2.3 HOW TO WRITE A NOTICE

An effective notice follows some principles in its diction and layout.

The language of a notice should be brief. Make it a rule to use no more words than are needed to make your meaning clear. For example, when "for" is enough to express the meaning, do not use "for the purpose of".

Brief, however, should not be achieved at the cost of completeness. A notice should be complete in its contents. For example, a notice of "Lost" should include what has been lost, when and where it was lost, as well as how the owner can be contacted.

The information provided by a notice should be clear. Use simple words instead of "big" words to make it easy to get the meaning across to the reader. For example, "chance" may be preferable to "opportunity".

A notice should be laid out in such a way that it is attractive to the reader. For example, its title is usually printed in bold in the middle of the first line. The main information such as activity, time and place is also made distinct. Sometimes pictures are used to make the notice more attractive.

Hereunder are some useful expressions for notice writing.

* It's hereby proclaimed that the board of directors has decided to dismiss Mr. ... from the post of ...
* This is to announce the establishment of a new branch of our company in ... with Mr. ... in charge.
* A meeting of department deans will be held in the first meeting room on ...
* All ... are expected to attend the meeting.
* It's hereby proclaimed that the board of directors has decided to dismiss Mr. ... from the post of ...
* It is hereby announced that upon the decision of the board of directors ... is appointed ...
* ... is not an employee of ... and this company will not be responsible for his actions.
* We have the pleasure to announce that, on ... our two firms of ... hitherto carrying on business

at ... respectively, will amalgamate under the style of ... which is located at ...

* Please be informed that from ... the business hitherto carried on in the name of ... will be continued under the style of ...
* We regret that the ... will be closed from May 21-30 for redecoration.
* Customers can still do their shopping at a temporary location at ...
* We apologize to customers for any inconvenience caused.
* A visit has been arranged for ... to ...
* Anyone who lost ... in ... please come the ... to claim it.
* I gratefully acknowledge my indebtedness to ...
* We look forward to your continued support.
* Quiet / Silence / Keep Quiet
* No Smoking / Smoking Not Allowed
* Keep off the Grass
* No Parking
* Don't Dump Rubbish Here
* No Admittance without a Pass
* Please Keep Hands Off
* School About, No Honking
* Be Careful
* Wet Paint
* Reduce Speed Now
* Speed Limit: 60 km/h
* Attention, Sharp Turn Ahead
* Inflammables—Keep Away from Fire
* Fragile, Don't Drop
* Keep Away from Moisture
* Don't Touch High-Tension Wire
* Glass, Attention
* Handle with Care
* This Side Up
* Not for Sale
* House to Let
* Night Bell
* Staff Members Only

2.4 SAMPLE NOTICES

Sample 2 (1)

April 16, 2021

Dear Sirs,

This is to announce the establishment of a new branch of our company in Chicago, with Mr. Sun Zhigang in charge.

We wish to avail ourselves of this opportunity to express our thanks to you for your cooperation with us in the past and hope that the setting-up of this branch will enable us to be of better service to you in the future.

Very truly yours,
Zhang Jun
Managing Director

Sample 2 (2)

Bargain

Opening of Siji Bookstore

A Special Introductory Offer

15% discount

This offer applies to all purchases over $50

Between March 1st and April 30th, 2021

For more information contact:

Siji Bookstore

Zhongshan Road

Nanjing, 210000

Tel: (025) 87843529

Sample 2 (3)

Lost

I lost a copy of *Business English Writing* in the reading room of the library yesterday. Will the finder please ring me up to fetch it back?

Tel: 54678228

Michelle Browne
April 15th, 2021

Sample 2 (4)

Found

Anyone who lost a wallet in the restaurant of the International Hotel this morning, in which there are some documents, tickets, money and some other things, please come to the Front Desk of the Hotel to claim it.

The Front Desk
International Hotel
May 15, 2021

Sample 2 (5)

Dean Meeting

The routine meeting of department deans will be held in the first meeting room on Thursday, at 9:00 a.m on October 18. All department deans are expected to attend the meeting.

The President Office

October 14, 2021

Sample 2 (6)

Lecture

By

Professor Larry Brown

From Columbia University

On

Cross-cultural Communication

At Room 101, Yingdong Hall

3:30 p.m., Thursday, October 11, 2021

Sample 2 (7)

Notice of Appointment

It is hereby announced that upon the decision of the board of directors Miss Yang Hong is appointed secretary of the managing director.

The Managing Director's Office

May 16, 2021

Sample 2 (8)

Notice of Discharge

It's hereby proclaimed that the board of directors has decided to dismiss Mr. George Smith from the post of chief of the Personnel Department.

The Director's Office

August 16, 2021

Sample 2 (9)

Temporary Relocation

We regret that the Four Spring Flower Shop will be closed from May 21-30 for redecoration. Customers can still do their shopping at a temporary location at 101 Zhongshan Road.

We apologize to customers for any inconvenience caused.

Four Spring Flower Shop

May 15, 2021

Sample 2 (10)

Merger of Business

  We have the pleasure to announce that, on and after February 18, 2021, our two firms of Huaying Trading Company and Qiangsheng Trading Company hitherto carrying on business at 16 Zhongshan Road and 28 Jiefang Road respectively, will amalgamate under the style of Huaqiang Trading Company, which is located at 29 Jianguo Road. We look forward to your continued support.

Huaying Trading Company
Qiangsheng Trading Company
January 31, 2021

Sample 2 (11)

A Small Flat Wanted

  I'm a student of Jiangsu University. I am in need of a small flat with a bedroom, a bathroom and a kitchen near the campus. The rent for such a flat will be negotiable. If interested, please call me at 8809826 or 13912345678.

Wang Hai
April 19, 2021

Sample 2 (12)

Acknowledgements

  One month ago when I was down with a serious problem with my heart, I came to this hospital for help. Dr. Wu Dong and Dr. Liu Xiaohong treated me with great care. With their help I am recovering fast and now am able to restart my work. I gratefully acknowledge my indebtedness to them.

Chen Dong
April 15, 2021

Sample 2 (13)

Safety Procedures in Case of Fire

If the bell rings:
(1) Go to the nearest fire exit. Do not run. Remain calm.
(2) Go down the stairs. Do not use the lift.
(3) Assemble outside the building in work group.
(4) Check your name against the name list.
(5) Wait until the bell stops ringing.
(6) Return to your office.

Sample 2 (14)

Toy Biz International 2019: New Delhi Toy Expo

Category: Gifts and Handicrafts
Date: 09 – 11 July, 2019
Location: Hall No. 12A, Pragati Maidan, Mathura Road, Railway Colony, New Delhi 110002 India
Organizer: Toy Association of India – 259, Anarkali Complex, Jhandewalan Ext., New Delhi 110055 India
Phone: +91-11-41540977, +91-11-43558149
Email: toyassociationofindia@gmail.com
Timings: 10:00 AM – 18:00 PM
Tickets: Free

Exhibition for Toys Industry

Toy Biz International 2019 is a premier event bringing with it the best in toy and child care industry. This event aspires to bring together the professional buyers, business visitors, importers, exporters, manufacturers, traders, whole sellers and end users to foster good business relations. Besides, this event also participates in and takes delegations to international fairs to promote Indian toy trade. Every year the Toy Association of India organizes **Toy Biz International B2B Fairs** for child related products to showcase the products of Indian toy manufacturers to both domestic and foreign buyers.

Toy Biz International 2019: Event Profile

Toy Biz International 2019 is the largest international toy trade show where the newest and hottest products in the children's entertainment marketplace are exhibited. It is on battery operated toys, board games and puzzles, craft toys, activity toys, dolls sets, hobbies sets, education toys, electrical toys, electronic toys, gift items, inflatable toys, mechanical toys, plastic toys, ride on toys, soft toys, stuffed toys, wooden toys, metal toys, etc.

Sample 2 (15)

Vice CEO

Tasks and responsibilities:

- Responsible for building up administrative routines in the establishment phase and daily administration in production phase;
- Managing the finance and bookkeeping department, incl. overall responsibility for operation of an efficient accounting/bookkeeping function, daily accounting tasks and reporting both to Chinese authorities and to management in China and abroad;
- Preparing monthly and yearly reports to HQ in Denmark, preparing statutory accounts, budgeting, developing internal processes, cost accounting, etc.;
- Preparing General Ledger, accounts receivable and accounts payable as well as controlling cash flow;

> - Being a member of the company's management team;
> - Report to the CEO.
>
> Qualifications:
> - Certified accountant or other relevant university degree;
> - At least 3-year relevant work experience in a private production company;
> - Familiarity with handling of import-export procedures, VAT, and with relevant local laws, regulations, and legal matters;
> - Experience in accounting management systems—ERP-systems;
> - Excellent language skills in both spoken and written English.
>
> Contact:
> Application with CV's in English and Chinese, along with salary requirements, should be e-mailed to hr@asiabase.com no later than March 14, 2021.

2.5 NOTES

(1) Language in an effective notice usually follows the principles stated below:
- Both the person who wrote the notice and the person whom the notice addressed to should be named in third person.
- Use some fixed sentence patterns such as "This is to announce…"
- Use peculiar spelling such as Shop'*til U* Drop.

(2) the notice giving full message of information　发布信息的通知

(3) the notice giving a warning or an instruction　给予警告或指示的通知

(4) notice in the format of mail　信函式通知

(5) notice in the format of leaflet　传单式通知

(6) notice in the format of poster　海报式通知

2.6 COMMUNICATION LABORATORY

A. Give a brief answer to the following questions.

(1) What are the functions of a notice?

(2) What are the characteristics of a notice?

(3) How can a notice be made effective?

B. Case Study

Write notices according to the following situations:

(1) The board of directors has decided to appoint Mr. Wu Dong as the Sales Manager.

(2) The General Manager asks all department managers to attend the routine sales meeting.

(3) The Spring Festival is coming. There will be a seven-day holiday.

(4) The English Department is going to hold a party to celebrate the coming New Year.

(5) Mr. Harris Yang from Harvard University will deliver a speech on Sino-US relations.

Unit 3 Invitations

Invitations are very common in our daily life. We may, on behalf of our company, invite our business contacts to a dinner, a party or some other activities. On these occasions, invitations should be sent in advance.

When an invitation is received, the guest invited, whether accepting the invitation or not, should reply immediately. In the reply, it should be stated clear whether he/she will be present or not. However, if "Regrets only" is written in an invitation, it requires a reply only if the guest invited cannot attend the gathering.

3.1 CATEGORIES OF INVITATIONS

Based on their different forms, invitations fall into two categories: invitation letters and invitation cards. An invitation letter resembles a business letter. Its wording is usually conversational, as though the writer were extending the invitation orally. Invitation cards, by comparison, are more formal than invitation letters in that they are fixed in structure pattern. Besides, compared with an invitation letter, there are usually fewer words in an invitation card, which provides only important information of the gathering and leaves out the details.

With the simplification of social contact codes, invitation letters are more widely used. However, on some formal occasions, it is still necessary to send invitation cards.

3.2 THE LAYOUT OF INVITATIONS

Invitation cards and invitation letters are different in their layouts.

3.2.1 Invitation Card

An invitation card usually consists of eight lines. In the first line is the full name of the invitation writer, followed in the second line by the phrase "request the pleasure of". In the third line comes the full name of the guest invited and in the fourth line the phrase "company at …". The date, the hour and the place of the gathering are written respectively in the fifth, sixth and seventh line. The eighth line is optional, depending on whether a reply is needed. If so, "R. S. V. P." (French abbreviation for "Please reply") or "Regrets only" will be written in this line. Sometimes the requirements for dress are also stated in the last line. The most commonly used phrases in this respect are "Dress Informal", "Dress Optional", "Long Suit", "Day Dress", "Black Tie" and "White Tie".

The reply to an invitation card should also follow a fixed pattern. It usually consists of seven lines. In the first line is the full name of the guest invited, followed in the second line by the phrase "accept with pleasure of" or "regret that ... prevents his acceptance of". Then comes the phrase "... 's (the writer's name) kind invitation" in the third line and "to ... (the gathering)" in the fourth line. The date, the hour and the place of the gathering are written respectively in the fifth, sixth and seventh line.

3.2.2 Invitation Letter

An invitation letter does not need to follow any rigid pattern. However, it should include the purpose of the invitation, the date, time, and place of the gathering and often the hope that the guest invited can attend the gathering.

In the letter reply to an invitation letter, the guest invited should first express gratitude and happiness for being invited. In the case of acceptance, it should be stated that the invited will be present on time. If the invited cannot be present at the gathering, the regret over it should be expressed and a sound reason should be given.

Hereunder are some expressions that may be useful in invitation writing.

* We would/should be (very) pleased/delighted/happy if you could ...
* We are planning/giving/having ... at ... on ...
* ... requests the honor of your presence at ... to be held in ... on ... from ... to ... p.m.
* ... cordially invites the pleasure of Mr. ... to ...
* You and ... are cordially invited to ...
* We are giving a party on ... to celebrate ... and would like you and ... to come.
* Could you and ... come to ... on ... at ... ?
* We take great pleasure in inviting you to attend the conference.
* I am honored that you should invite me to ...
* We are looking forward to seeing you.
* We (sincerely) hope ...
* We do hope you can join us.
* We do hope you will be able to spare the time to share this occasion with us.
* We are awaiting your arrival.
* Let us know as soon as possible if you can come and tell me when you will be able to come.
* Please reply to ... no later than ...
* Please confirm your participation at your earliest convenience.
* I hope you are not too busy to come.
* I accept with pleasure your invitation to ... on ... I will be there on time.
* It is very kind of you to invite us to ... and we would like to come.
* Thank you very much for your kind invitation. I should love to come and am looking forward to seeing you.
* Nothing could give us greater pleasure than accepting your kind invitation.
* I am looking forward to meeting all of you.

* I should love to come very much, but unfortunately, a previous engagement prevents me from coming.
* I regret that I have another engagement at this time and will not be able to come.
* I appreciate very much your kind invitation, but I regret to say that I have made another appointment at that time.
* Please accept my sincere regret at not being able to join you on that day.
* Unfortunately, it will be impossible for me to be present at your dinner party.
* I hope I shall manage to find time to come next time.
* I wish I could be present, but owing to being away on vacation, I regret to inform you that I will not be able to come.
* Your traveling expenses will be borne by us.
* Sorry for the inconvenience caused.

3.3 SAMPLE INVITATIONS

Sample 3 (1)

An invitation to a dinner
Mr. and Mrs. John Hobart request the pleasure of Mr. and Mrs. Robert Silver's company at dinner on Tuesday, March the Sixth at seven o'clock p.m. Grand Hotel
R.S.V.P.   Tel: 35792684

Sample 3 (2)

Accepting an invitation
Mr. and Mrs. Robert Silver accept with pleasure Mr. and Mrs. John Hobart's kind invitation to dinner on Tuesday, March the Sixth at seven o'clock p.m. Grand Hotel

Sample 3 (3)

Declining an invitation
Mr. and Mrs. Robert Silver regret that a previous engagement prevents their acceptance of Mr. and Mrs. John Hobart's kind invitation to dinner on Tuesday, March the Sixth at seven o'clock p.m. Grand Hotel

Sample 3 (4)

An invitation letter to a reception
September 10, 2021 Dear Mr. Jordan, 　　This is to invite you to the National Day reception to be held in the City Hall at 6:00 p.m. on Tuesday, September 28. 　　As the National Day is approaching, we are giving this reception to express our appreciation and gratitude to the foreign experts here for your help with the development of the city. 　　We sincerely hope you can attend. Please let us know as soon as possible if you can come. Sincerely yours, Li Nan

Sample 3 (5)

An invitation letter to a dinner party
May 20, 2021 Dear Mrs. Smith, 　　We should be very much pleased if you and Mr. Smith would come to dinner on Sunday, May 30 at 7 o'clock. Many of our friends will come. We do hope you will be able to spare the time to share this occasion with us. Truly yours, Elizabeth Jones

Sample 3（6）

Accepting an invitation to a dinner party
May 24, 2021 Dear Mrs. Jones, 　　Thank you for your kind invitation. My husband and I would be delighted to come to dinner. It is quite a long time since we met last. We are looking forward to seeing you then. 　　　　　　　　　　　　　　　　　　　　　　　　　　Truly yours, 　　　　　　　　　　　　　　　　　　　　　　　　　　Susan Smith

Sample 3（7）

Declining an invitation to a dinner party
May 24, 2021 Dear Mrs. Jones, 　　Thank you very much for your kind invitation. 　　My husband and I would like very much to be present at your dinner party, but unfortunately we will be traveling abroad at that time. 　　It was sweet of you to invite us, and we are looking forward to seeing you at another time. 　　　　　　　　　　　　　　　　　　　　　　　　　　Truly yours, 　　　　　　　　　　　　　　　　　　　　　　　　　　Susan Smith

Sample 3（8）

Being unable to attend a dinner after having accepted the invitation
May 24, 2021 Dear Mrs. Jones, 　　Your dinner party of May 30 sounds so pleasant, but now I suddenly find that I cannot come as I promised. My daughter is seriously ill and it requires at least eight days of constant care. She is already getting well now, but unfortunately I am sorry the time for dinner had to be right now. 　　I am sorry for the inconvenience caused. Hope we can get together at another time. 　　　　　　　　　　　　　　　　　　　　　　　　　　Truly yours, 　　　　　　　　　　　　　　　　　　　　　　　　　　Susan Smith

Sample 3 (9)

Change of schedule for a dinner party

May 24, 2021

Dear Mrs. Smith,

    It is with great regret that I must write to tell you that our dinner party, planned for Sunday, May 30 must be postponed until June 1. My daughter is seriously ill and it requires at least eight days of constant care. She is already getting well now, but I am sorry the dinner has to be put off. I hope that you and Mr. Smith can come instead on Friday, June 1.

    Looking forward to seeing you.

Truly yours,

Elizabeth Jones

Sample 3 (10)

Invitation to a conference

April 21, 2021

Dear Mr. Anderson,

    The 15th Annual Conference on English Teaching will be held in Nanjing from Monday July 5 to Wednesday July 7. We take great pleasure in inviting you to attend the conference.

    We are hoping to have a half-day session on task-based teaching and because of your high reputation in this field, we would like to invite you to lead the session. If you accept we shall, of course, pay you a fee plus expenses.

    Would you please let me know as soon as possible if you can accept and also which day and time would be convenient for you? If you need any equipment, we can have them available.

    We were wondering if the session could include a talk by you; the members could form groups for discussion and to prepare questions for you to answer at the end of the session. Of course, if you would prefer different arrangements we shall fit in with them.

    I do hope you will be able to accept our invitation.

Sincerely yours,

Zhang Xiuying

Sample 3 (11)

Accepting an invitation to a conference

April 30, 2021

Dear Ms. Zhang,

    Thank you for your letter of April 21. I am honored that you should invite me to lead the session on publicity.

    I will be available on Monday July 5 and suggest that we start at 2:00 p.m.

No special equipment will be necessary, but I would ask that conference members have paper and a pen or pencil.

The structure of the session which you outlined would be suitable to me.

I look forward to meeting you at the conference.

Sincerely yours,
John Anderson

Sample 3 (12)

Declining an invitation to a conference

April 30, 2021

Dear Ms. Zhang,

Thank you for your letter of April 21. I am honored that you should invite me to lead the session on publicity. But heavy official duties prevent me from having the pleasure to join you at that time. For this I am very sorry. I hope I shall manage to find time to come next year.

Kindest regards to you.

Sincerely yours,
John Anderson

Sample 3 (13)

An invitation to a wedding ceremony

May 10, 2021

Dear Nancy,

Li Ming and I are going to have our wedding on June 8, at the International Hotel at 12 o'clock. It is a traditional Chinese wedding. We would be very happy if you and your husband could come.

We are looking forward to seeing you.

Yours truly,
Lin Hong

Sample 3 (14)

An invitation of visit

June 15, 2021

Dear Mr. McWilliams,

We take great interest in your letter of June 9, 2021 in which you expressed your hope to make a personal visit here to promote our cooperation in the future.

Cherishing the same hope for furtherance of our business relations, we quite agree with you that a discussion between us in person is helpful and necessary. Since you think that it is convenient for you to go abroad in September, we would like to suggest that you come to attend the session of the Chinese Export Commodities Fair, in Guangzhou, to be held from October 15 to November 4, 2021. The responsible members and sales representatives of this corporation will be there to meet you. You may have a splendid chance to examine a wide range of our export commodities as well as new varieties for your selection. On-the-spot business talks and discussions will be conducted there, with the participation of the relevant manufacturers, if necessary. We shall of course be happy to welcome you to Nanjing after you visit the fair, if so directed.

We shall ask the Fair to send you an invitation, provided you will make a visit and inform us of your intention.

Yours sincerely,
Ma Wenjun

Sample 3 (15)

Reply to an invitation of visit

June 25, 2021

Dear Mr. Ma,

I have received with thanks your letter dated June 15. Your proposal is of great interest to me. As mentioned by you, it will benefit both of us a lot by a discussion in person. I have decided to visit the session of the Chinese Export Commodities Fair, in Guangzhou on October 16.

I hope this visit will further our business relations.

Looking forward to seeing you.

Yours sincerely,
John McWilliams

Sample 3 (16)

An invitation to an anniversary party

October 20, 2021

Dear Prof. Yang,

On Tuesday, October 26 all the faculty members of Jiangsu University will celebrate the twentieth anniversary of the school founding.

We have decided to have a party in honor of the occasion on October 26 at seven p.m. at the Multi-function Hall. We are looking forward to seeing you.

In order to make proper reservations, will you please send your acceptance to the attention of Professor Liu no later than October 23?

Sincerely yours,
Yu Fang

3.4 NOTES

(1) invitation card 请柬
(2) Regrets Only: Please let us know if you cannot attend.
(3) RSVP: Please let us know if you plan to attend.
(4) Dress Informal/Dress Optional/Lounge Suit/Day Dress 衣着随便
(5) Black Tie 礼服外套、黑色领结、衬衫、西裤、马甲、皮鞋、口袋巾等
(6) White Tie 宴会着装最高等级,包括黑色燕尾服、白色领结、白色马甲、翼领白色礼服衬衫、黑色礼服西裤、黑色漆皮皮鞋、白色口袋巾、礼服帽等

3.5 COMMUNICATION LABORATORY

A. Give a brief answer to the following questions.
   (1) What should an invitation include?
   (2) What are the differences between an invitation card and an invitation letter?
   (3) Describe the structure of an invitation card.

B. Case Study

   Write invitations and replies according to the following situations:
   (1) The English Department is giving a small dinner party to celebrate Teacher's Day.
   (2) Invite one foreign teacher to your birthday party.
   (3) One of your American friends is traveling in China with his family. Invite them to a dinner in a restaurant with Chinese specialty.
   (4) Invite a foreign professor to give students of English Department a lecture on cross-cultural communication.

Unit 4 Toasts

The English term "toast" has been traced to the 17th century, and had reference at first to the custom of drinking to the ladies. In Stuart times, it was the practice to put a piece of toast in the wine cup from belief that it improved the flavor of the wine. Now it has evolved into the custom of delivering a few words in the presence of a group of people at a party just before drinking to the welfare of the person(s) being honored, or to the interest of everybody present at the party.

Toasts can be made when a dinner party is being held on almost any occasions like wedding ceremonies, gatherings of family members or friends, birthday parties, wedding anniversaries, retirement ball, inaugurating ball, state banquet, graduating ceremonies, opening ceremonies of all kinds, etc. Owing to the different occasions they are made, toasts can be used for different purposes.

Toasts can be delivered to celebrate the successes people have achieved in their business and studies. A toast can be given when a new member is recruited to an organization of celebrity, when a friend is elected into the board of directors, when a colleague is promoted, or when a new president is nominated.

At wedding ceremonies, toasts are addressed to the bride and groom for their happy union as a result of their love. They can also be addressed to the newly married couples to express the speakers' wishes about their happiness after their marriage. On wedding anniversaries, toasts are made to celebrate the endurance of love and friendship between the couples over the elapsing of time. At birthday parties, toasts are always made to celebrate people's maturity and long life. Expressions about future success and happiness are also to be embedded within birthday toasts.

On occasions when people are retiring from their jobs, toasts can be given to celebrate their freedom in future. Words of praise can be given about their past contribution. Words of regrets or losses can be added in their honor to show their significance in their jobs. The same is true with toasts made at other farewell dinner parties.

At dinner parties given by a government to welcome visiting officials or heads of states from other countries, toasts are presented mainly for the purpose of promoting friendly relationships between countries. Dinner parties hosted by companies are usually a great occasion for the presidents of these companies to express their gratitude in their toasts for the contribution done by their employees. Expectations about future prosperity that will lead to joint success will always be emphasized in toasts made on such an occasion.

Whatever the occasions, toasts are drafted to guide people into a bright future by praising past achievements and belittling past losses. Personal welfares like health, achievements, love and friendship, happiness, are just what count most in toasts of any kind.

4.1 THE LAYOUT OF TOASTS

A toast normally consists of two elements: a statement of good wishes and the response of the audience by drinking. But in practice, the statement of good wishes is always presented in the format of speeches.

A toast is generally delivered in three parts, namely the greeting, the body, and the proposal to toast the persons to be honored.

The greeting part of a toast aims at drawing the audience's attention. It is usually unacceptable to draw the audience's attention by hitting glasses. The speaker may stand up, look around, and open the toast by greeting the audience. The body can be further divided into three parts. The body part should first of all delineate the relationship between the speaker and the person(s) to whose welfare the toast is delivered. This part is quite important because it authorizes the speaker to proceed with the toast. After this, the speaker should move on to make a review about the history, mostly the achievements or contribution of the person(s) being honored. If it is a toast addressed to visiting officials from another country, the review should be made about the diplomatic relationships between the two countries, as well as the achievements made by people in the country where those visiting officials come. Finally, the speaker should move back to what is happening, namely, what has occasioned the gathering.

The proposal is the climax of a toast. In this part, the speaker summons up the audience's ardor and passion to drink for a list of benefits bestowed to the person(s) being honored, or to drink for the benefit of a list of people to be honored. After the enumeration of a list of benefits or a list of people, the speaker will call for the response from the audience by calling out "Cheers!" with his/her glass held out forward simultaneously. Or the speaker will raise his/her glass at the completion of his enumeration of a list of benefits or a list of people, leaving a pause just long enough for the audience to respond.

Therefore, a toast should include the following information:
- By whom is the toast proposed?
- Whom is the toast addressed to?
- What is the relationship between the toast giver and the person(s) being honored?
- On what occasion is the toast delivered?
- Why does the person in question deserve the honor or what is the person's glorious

history that deserves praise?
- What benefits are proposed?

These should be organized in the manner shown in the following examples:

Format 1

> Mr. President Hu, Madam Liu:
>
> Laura and I are honored to welcome you and your delegation to the White House. It's a pleasure to have you here, along with our other distinguished guests.
>
> China is home to an ancient civilization, and it is helping to shape the modern world. In a single generation, China's economy has moved from isolation and stagnation to engagement and expansion. As China has grown, our two peoples have come to known one another better.
>
> Thirty-five years ago this month, the Chinese government welcomed the United States ping-pong team to Beijing. It's an event that marked the beginning of renewal—renewed cultural exchanges between our two nations. Today Chinese athletes compete professionally in the United States, and Americans appreciate the opportunity to see them play.
>
> In 2008, China will welcome athletes from all over the world as your great nation hosts the summer Olympics. Beijing will showcase China's transformation and demonstrate China's commitment to the international institutions that make fair and peaceful competition possible for all nations.
>
> Mr. President, I thank you for the constructive and candid conversations we had this morning. I appreciate the opportunity to expand the dialogue between our two great nations. And Mr. President, I'm pleased to offer a toast to you and to your gracious wife, and to the people of China.

This is a toast delivered by President Bush to visiting Chinese President Hu in 2005. In this toast, the toast is addressed to Chinese President Hu Jintao and his delegation, as well as all the Chinese people as a whole. The toast giver is the American counterpart of Chinese President Hu Jintao, with whom he has held some constructive conversations about Sino-American relationships. It is delivered at the state banquet in the White House to welcome the visiting Chinese President and his delegation. The toast is proposed by President Bush, his wife and all other American representatives at the dinner party to honor President Hu and all other Chinese people for their contribution to the healthy development of Sino-American relationship and world peace, as well as the friendship between the two countries.

Format 2

> OK, everyone.
>
> Just a few words about Bill's retirement.
>
> When I told people I was going to make a retirement speech today they got quite excited ... until I explained that it wasn't me who was retiring.
>
> Bill, you were here long before I joined the organization. In fact, I reckon you know more stories

> than anyone about what's happened here over the years. Like that time a horse got into the warehouse a few years back. You were the only one who was brave enough to go in and get it out. What amazed everyone though was when you came out riding on its back!
>
> Anyway Bill, we would all like to wish you the best of fortune for the future. If we get any problems with livestock we'll call you, but other than that have a great time with the fishing.
>
> Many thanks for all you've done for us, Bill and best of luck for a long and happy retirement.

This is a retirement toast delivered in a much more casual manner to honor the retirement of Bill. The addresser is one of Bill's colleagues. This toast is proposed to all present at the retirement ball to express their congratulation on the retirement of Bill, as well as their blessings for him. In this toast, the addresser does not review the glorious past of the person being honored. Instead, he draws a comparison between Bill and an old horse which is just so amiable and assiduous a figure that deserves people's admiration.

Format 3

> (Tom stands up, looking around and holding up his glass)
> Now I want to ask you to join me in a toast to Grandpa in remaining happy and young forever!

This is a toast addressed at a family gathering to Grandpa. This is a simplified format of toast in which the addresser leaves out many of the elements found in Format 1 and Format 2.

Since toasts are to be delivered before an audience in social gatherings, toasts are similar to public speeches in many ways. Both of them are prepared in advance and are presented orally to the audience.

But toasts are somewhat different from speeches. A toast is normally a statement of good wishes that calls for the audience's responses by lifting their glasses to drink, whereas a speech can focus on any topics other than good wishes. A speech can be delivered both at dinner parties and at meetings with the purpose of informing the conventioneers of given topics. Toasts, on the other hand, are always addressed at dinner parties or balls to specific individuals in an effort to celebrate the individuals' birthday, wedding ceremonies, wedding anniversaries, retirement, and so on. In a word, toasts are just statements about the welfare of the individuals being addressed to. Furthermore, toasts are usually shorter than speeches.

In view of the similarities and differences between toasts and speeches, toasts can be prepared and delivered as speeches in miniature. In many cases, a toast is to be made at the end of a speech. Then it can be called a toast speech. For these reasons, toasts can take the format of speeches.

4.2 THE PLANNING OF TOASTS

A successfully written toast speech always follows strict organization of different sorts of information pertinent in honoring the person(s) in question. The steps in organizing a formal toast are:

a) Identifying the person(s) being honored;
b) Addressing the audience;
c) Specifying the occasion to deliver the toast;
d) Specifying the qualification of the addresser;
e) Reviewing the achievements and contributions made by the person(s) being honored;
f) Calling for the audience to join the addresser in making a toast to the person(s) in question by holding up his/her glass.

Because toasts are usually delivered at boisterous dinner parties or balls, the addresser usually stands up, looks around, and holds up his/her glass to call the audience's attention before starting to address the person(s) being honored and other guests present at the parties or balls. The toast is generally realized by drinking the wine.

At informal gatherings, toasts can be prepared and delivered with the omission of some parts of the information listed above in formal toasts. For example, the toast in Format 3 just leaves out item c), item d) and item e).

4.3 THE TONE OF TOASTS

The toast speech should be conveyed in such a manner that it is easy to persuade both the person(s) being honored and the audience being present. To do this, the speaker should express his/her wishes in a sincere way. Improperly conveyed speeches may even bring the audience into fury and commotion.

The enumerating of the achievements and contributions made by the person(s) being honored should be presented in a tone to convey the addresser's appreciation and admiration.

The tone of the toasts is determined both by the formality of the occasions and the popularity of the person(s) being honored. The tone of the toast delivered at a state banquet to treat foreign guests will always arouse among the audience awe and admiration, whereas a toast made by a good friend at an informal gathering can be interesting and humorous, as exemplified in Format 2.

4.4 PRESENTATION OF CONTENT

The presentation of toasts should also follow some principles listed as follows:

(1) Brief and Simple in Diction

Since a toast is intended to be read before an audience, the language of it should be brief. Difficult words and complex sentence structures will often prove difficult for the audience to catch the meaning of the toast. Furthermore, simple words combined in brief sentences will be helpful for building up the force of the toast, which in turn will be effective in summoning up the audience's passion and ardor.

(2) Pertinent in Contents

When reviewing the history of the person(s) being addressed, the speaker should just tell suitable incidents. Past failures or scandals about the honored person(s) will not only bring about great discomfort or shame, but also ruin the gathering. Therefore, before writing a toast speech, the speaker should make a survey about the person(s) to be honored and select what match the person(s) and occasion to be celebrated.

(3) Using Nonverbal Language

Nonverbal language plays an essential role in delivering a toast. Before starting the toast, the addresser normally stands up, looks around, and holds up his/her glass of wine. During the process of the delivery, the addresser should make constant eye contact with the audience to show his sincerity and friendliness, instead of keeping his/her eyes on the script of the toast speech. At the close of the toast, the addresser should again raise high his/her glass of wine in calling for the response from the audience.

4.5 EFFECTIVE TOAST CHECKLIST

The following is a list of points to check when you write a toast speech.
- Have you used the correct toast format for the right occasion?
- Have you qualified yourself in making the toast?
- Have you made clear whom you are honoring?
- Have you included all relevant information to show that the person being honored deserves the audience's respect?
- Is your writing style direct and simple?
- Have you written appropriately to your audience?
- Have you achieved the correct tone?
- Have you checked spelling, grammar and punctuation?

4.6 SAMPLE TOASTS

Sample 4 (1): A State Dinner Toast

Speech by President Xi Jinping, also general secretary of the CPC Central Committee and chairman of the Central Military Commission, at the reception in celebration of the 70th anniversary of the founding of the People's Republic of China (October 1, 2019)

Ladies and Gentlemen,

Comrades and Friends,

In this golden season of autumn, we are gathered here to mark the 70th anniversary of the founding of the People's Republic of China. For the Chinese people of all ethnic groups and Chinese sons and daughters at home and abroad, this is a joyful moment—a moment to celebrate the 70th birthday of our great People's Republic and to salute the epic progress of our motherland during the past seven decades.

Over the past 70 years, under the strong leadership of the Communist Party of China (CPC), the Chinese people, with great courage and relentless exploration, have successfully opened the path of socialism with Chinese characteristics. Along this path, we have ushered in a new era. Having caught up with the world in great strides, we are now marching forward at the forefront of the times with boundless energy!

Over the past 70 years, the Chinese people, with perseverance and strenuous efforts, have made development achievements that are the marvel of the world. Absolute poverty, which has haunted the Chinese nation for thousands of years, will soon become a thing of the past. This will be a great miracle in human history!

Over the past 70 years, the Chinese people, upholding an independent foreign policy of peace, have forged ahead along the path of peaceful development. Guided by the Five Principles of Peaceful Coexistence, we have deepened friendship and cooperation with other countries and made an important contribution to building a community with a shared future for mankind and advancing the noble cause of peace and development for humanity!

Seventy years are but a fleeting moment in human history. But for the Chinese people, for our nation, these have been 70 years of epoch-making changes. The Chinese nation has realized a tremendous transformation: it has stood up, grown rich and is becoming stronger; it has come to embrace the brilliant prospects of national renewal. This phenomenal transformation brings infinite pride to every son and daughter of the Chinese nation!

Here on behalf of the CPC Central Committee and the State Council, I pay high tribute to the Chinese people of all ethnic groups and all CPC members, to officers and men of the People's Liberation Army and members of the armed police, and to all the other political parties and personages with no party affiliations in China! I wish to convey sincere greetings to fellow Chinese in the Hong Kong and Macao Special Administrative Regions, in Taiwan and residing abroad! I also wish to express heartfelt thanks to all the countries and international friends who have given support and help to the development of New China!

Comrades and Friends!

Unity is iron and steel; unity is a source of strength. It is what has enabled the Chinese people and the Chinese nation to move forward against all risks and challenges, from one victory to another.

In our new journey, we must hold high the banner of unity and rally closely around the CPC Central Committee. We must cement the great unity of all our ethnic groups, and strengthen the great unity of all Chinese sons and daughters at home and abroad and of all political parties, organizations, ethnic groups, social strata and fronts. We must maintain the close bond between the CPC and the people and promote patriotism. Thus we will create an unparalleled force that will power the ship of our national renewal to clip waves and reach its destination.

Comrades and Friends!

We will continue to fully and faithfully implement the principles of "One Country, Two Systems", "Hong Kong people administering Hong Kong", "Macao people administering Macao" and a high degree of autonomy. We will act in strict accordance with the Constitution and the Basic Laws. We are confident that with the full backing of the motherland and the concerted efforts of our fellow Chinese in Hong Kong and Macao who love the motherland as well as their communities, Hong Kong and Macao will prosper and progress alongside the mainland and embrace an even brighter future!

We will uphold the one-China principle and the "1992 Consensus", promote the peaceful development of relations across the Taiwan Strait, and deepen cross-Strait economic and cultural exchanges and cooperation to the benefit of people on both sides. The complete reunification of the motherland is an inevitable trend; it is what the greater national interests entail and what all Chinese people aspire for. No one and no force can ever stop it!

We will hold high the banner of peace, development, cooperation and mutual benefit, and keep firmly to the path of peaceful development. We will stay committed to opening-up and work with people in all countries to build a community with a shared future for mankind, and to create a world bathed in peace and development.

Comrades and Friends,

The Chinese people are great people, the Chinese nation is a great nation, and Chinese civilization is a great civilization. History will shed light on the future, and our journey ahead will be a long one. We are convinced that the Chinese people and the Chinese nation, with a proud civilization spanning over five millennia and great accomplishments during the past 70-year history of New China, will write a more brilliant chapter in our new journey toward the realization of the Two Centenary Goals and the Chinese Dream of great national renewal.

Now please join me in a toast:

To the 70th anniversary of the founding of the People's Republic of China;

To the prosperity and strength of China and the happiness and well-being of the Chinese people of all ethnic groups;

To the friendship and cooperation between the people of China and all other countries; and

To the health of all the guests, comrades and friends present.

Cheers!

Sample 4 (2): A Return Toast

President Hu: (as translated)

Mr. President, and Mrs. Bush, distinguished guests, ladies and gentlemen, dear friends: First of all, I wish to express on behalf of my wife and my colleagues and in my own way, my sincere thanks to you, Mr. President, and Mrs. Bush for your thoughtful arrangements and gracious hospitality. I also wish to thank the President and Mrs. Bush for giving me this important opportunity to renew my friendship with old friends and make new ones at this grand welcoming luncheon.

Over the years, all of you present here have worked to promote the friendship between our two peoples and promote China-US relations. On behalf of the Chinese government and the people, I wish to hereby extend our warm greetings and best wishes to you and through you to all the Americans who care about and support the growth of China-US relations.

On this visit, I have keenly felt the warm friendship of the American people towards the Chinese people. In the past, the Chinese and the Americans sympathized with, helped and supported each other. We will never forget the invaluable support given to us by the American government and people in our struggle against fascist aggression. We will always cherish our profound friendship with the American people forged over the long years.

In the past 27 years, since the establishment of our diplomatic ties, China-US relations have, as a whole, moved ahead, despite difficulties and problems. Recent years, in particular, have seen major progress in building constructive and cooperative China-US relations. We have carried out fruitful cooperation in wide-ranging areas, including trade, counterterrorism, nonproliferation, and on major international and regional issues. This has expanded the common strategic interests of our two countries, and promoted world peace and development.

As history has shown, to ensure the continued growth of China-US relations represents the shared desire of our two peoples and meets the fundamental interests of our two countries and peoples.

As we look across the world, we find ourselves in an era of both opportunities and challenges. China and the United States, respectively being the largest developing country and the largest developed country, share growing common interests, expanding areas for cooperation and increasing historical responsibilities. China-US relations have gone far beyond the bilateral context and have become increasingly global in nature. China and the United States are not only stakeholders, but they should also be constructive partners—be parties of constructive cooperation.

Just now, President Bush and I have concluded an in-depth exchange of views and reached a broad and important agreement on China-US relations, and regional and international issues of mutual interest. We agreed to maintain regular high-level exchanges and increase interactions at various levels. We agreed to deepen economic and trade cooperation, enhance dialogue on macroeconomic policies, and strengthen communication and coordination of major regional and international issues.

We also agreed to promote people-to-people exchanges, especially those among young people, and promote exchange and cooperation in cultural, educational, and other fields. In short, we are committed to increasing mutual trust, deepening cooperation, and advancing in an all-around way, the constructive and cooperative China-US relationship in the 21st century.

As you all know, China has, since the late 1970s, gone through major transformations in the process of reform and opening up. In the years to come, China will continue to make economic development a top priority, press ahead with the reform and the opening up program, promote its modernization drive, and endeavor to make life better for its 1.3 billion people.

China will keep firmly to the path of peaceful development and work unswervingly to safeguard world peace and promote common development. What has happened has proven, and it will continue to prove, that China's development has brought about prosperity and stability to the Chinese people, and peace and progress to people elsewhere in the world.

China will, as always, live in peace with other countries and work with them to promote mutually beneficial cooperation and common development, contributing even more to the lofty cause of peace and development and of mankind.

China-US relations now stand at a new historical juncture. Let me quote here the lines of a poem written by Du Fu, a great Chinese poet, in the Tang Dynasty, entitled "A View from the Top of Mount Tai", which reads something like this: "Climb up to the summit and see the mountains around and below we are."

We should view and handle our relations from a strategic and long-term perspective, keep to the common strategic interests of the two countries, enhance dialogue, mutual trust and cooperation, accommodate each other's interests, and properly address differences. By doing so, I'm confident that we can ensure the sound and steady growth of China-US relations and bring more benefits to both our two peoples and to people of other countries.

Now, please join me in a toast to the health of the President and Mrs. Bush, to the health of all friends present here today, to the friendship between the Chinese and the American peoples, and to the bright future for China-US relations.

(A toast is offered.)

(Applause)

Sample 4 (3): A Wedding Toast

Good evening, everyone.

What can I say about my son, Larry? Well, he's an extraordinary young man, living an extraordinary life for starters. He has always been extraordinary, in fact. And here are just a few samplings of a life that's long in texture, rich in accomplishment and ... well ... yes ... extraordinary.

Larry was the 3rd of three boys, coming after Joe and David. He had beautiful, golden blonde curls, a mischievous set of ice blue eyes, a sunny disposition and a competitive nature that was sharp and strong as steel.

He had no fear whatsoever. Before he could swim, he jumped into the deep end of a swimming pool and sank like a stone. He was blue when I pulled him out. Then he jumped right back in again.

He always wanted to be better, higher, bigger, faster. At 4, he was taken by his uncle to ride a real horse. But the horse was slow and Larry, perturbed as usual, demanded that his uncle "press the button and make the horse go faster".

Naturally, someone as fearless as Larry spent a lot of time in emergency rooms. Dislocated joints, sprained fingers and ankles were commonplace. Once he split his knee wide open. We were such regular customers that I used to get paranoid, worried that the doctors thought I was abusing my adorable little golden-haired hellion.

Tough as he was, he was never afraid to show affection. Even as a teenager, when he'd be cavorting with all of his buddies at the mall, if he saw me there he'd stop everything, come over and give me a great big hug. He did the same with his grandmother, too.

After college, he was bored and uncertain of what to do, so he decided to take off for Japan and a gig teaching English to Japanese businessmen. I didn't want my baby traipsing off to the other side of the world and I was very upset. But Larry is so smart. He actually wrote up a contract, promising me that he'd always be my baby—if I would let him go to Japan. I was charmed. I was moved. I was scared to death. But I signed the contract. He went to Japan and had the year of his life. In fact, I have to admit, the experience was wonderful. And, per the contract, I have him back. He is my baby for life.

He was the youngest firefighter hired in Vancouver. He's a self-taught contractor who, along with big brother Mike, bought a house, fixed it up and sold it 8 months later for a small fortune. He learned to drive big rig air brake trucks. He's a deep sea rescue expert and a Coast Guard volunteer. He played professional basketball—in Poland, yet.

And now, I lose my baby again. But not to Japan. Instead, to a lovely young woman. He met Thelma in 2006. She matured him, polished his edges, gave him a beautiful son, Billy, in January. They're very much in love and they're very good for each other. I wish them both a world of happiness—and a world of eternal love. Besides, no matter what, Larry will always be my baby. I have the signed contract to prove it.

Love, Mom

Sample 4 (4): A Best Man Toast at a Wedding

Good Evening.

My name is James, and on behalf of Matthew and Angie, I would like to thank you for attending this blessed event today! I have the double honor of acting as both Officiate and Best Man tonight, and am thrilled that I am with these two wonderful people as they begin this new chapter in their lives.

This is an especially eventful day because it offers Angie and Matthew each a second chance at happiness. What a wonderful day of hope and joy, peace and contentment.

Angie and Matthew have each walked many miles to be here together today, and this wedding is a joy to behold. I can speak for everyone in this room, when I say we all wish you the happiness that you deserve. We are so glad that you have found one another, and this day is a reminder that the best is yet to come.

Each of you has worked hard to get here today, and when life handed you difficulties, it did not make you bitter, it made you better. Your marriage to each other is a true triumph of hope over experience. It's been said that if marriage is to be a success, one should begin by marrying the right person. It's obvious that each of you is indeed marrying the right person today.

Angie and Matthew met as student and teacher when Angie was taking architecture classes. These two wonderful people, who know how to build homes, and bridges, and all sorts of other things, are blessed to know that any thing that is going to last a long time starts with a good foundation. Keeping these rules in mind, it is already clear that the foundation Ken and Angie have created for their life together is sturdy, and will withstand all the storms and sunny days ahead.

I don't think I've ever seen a couple who complement each other as much as these two do. Matthew is an intelligent, soft-spoken, organized and witty man. He is very well respected in his field of architecture, and he's just a generally all-round nice guy, too!

Angie is a dear, dear friend who has been on a spiritual journey to better herself and I would say she has had a remarkable quest. In her business, Angie focuses her architecture with a "healing" aspect (colors, material, placement of windows, doors, etc.). I have always been amazed at her ability to pull things together and transform the dull and ordinary into something extraordinary.

I enjoy watching Angie and Matthew challenge each other to continuously be better. They are very supportive of each other, and while they compete in the same field, they are never competitors. They are two people with a wonderful amount of synergy and they are a joy to know. Their family is rounded out by Cookie, their chocolate lab, and the three of them seem very content to be together!

They say that there is no surprise as magical as finding your life's mate later in life. You two must feel the magic, because it seems as if your happiness emanates from you on this very magical day!

I really feel that I would be remiss if I did not just give you a couple of pieces of advice. Primarily, though, Matthew, these are directed at you.

Never go to bed angry ... always stay up and argue.

Always remember the three little words ... "You're right, dear".

Keep the lid down, and the best way to remember your anniversary is to forget it once.

Let's raise our glasses as we toast this couple.

May you both live as long as you want. And never want as long as you live.

Sample 4 (5): Anniversary Toast for Grandparents

What an honor it is to speak at my grandparent's 60th anniversary. It's not often we get an opportunity to celebrate an event like this, so I think, first off, congratulations are in order.

60 years! Some day I hope I'll be able to say I even lived that long. But to be married! To actually live with another person for that length of time—it's remarkable. I mean, our parents had us out of the house after 18 years, and, admittedly, all of us kids had probably had enough of them by that time, but 60 years! This should win you a prize of some sort, shouldn't it?

Honestly, now, I know we don't get many opportunities to tell you, but you should realize how much of an inspiration your marriage is to all of us. It gives us all great pleasure celebrating the commitment you have shown one another in your lives, and you should know the influence of your love is not lost on this family. I'm sure part of the reason Mom and Dad have such a wonderful marriage is because, in this case, (mom/dad) grew up in a very loving household. Naturally, that spirit of love and support has been passed along to our generation.

Of course, as grandchildren we always revere what you've said. Some of our fondest memories from childhood revolve around them. What stands above all is the impression that you were always so happy to see us, always interested in what we were doing and thinking.

Later, as we grew up and began seeing you for the adults you are, we began appreciating all that you've done with your lives. [Granddad and Grandma] have very much become a symbol for the joys of leading a long and healthy life. You show us that life doesn't stop at any age, and that it keeps on getting better if you tackle it with the same energy and interest every day. Naturally, if you're lucky enough to have a partner there to share the experience, life will be all the more rich.

Having said that, I'd like to propose a toast to the couple who helps show us the way. Would you all raise your glasses and drink to [NAME & NAME], still, after all these years, the happy couple!

4.7 NOTES

(1) A speech generally comprises four parts: the heading, the greeting, the body, and the conclusion. The heading part of a speech refers to the topic to be discussed in the speech. The greeting part of a speech is presented to draw the audience's attention. The body part of a speech discusses in details to convey the speaker's opinion about the topic. The concluding part draws a conclusion of what has been talked about and thanks the audience for their attention.

(2) A return toast is one addressed back to the person who has just made a toast speech to honor you.

(3) Useful Expressions

1) ... have the honor to host ...
2) Now I'd like to propose a toast to ...
3) What an honor it is to speak at ... the 20th anniversary of ...
4) Let's raise our glasses as we toast this couple ...
5) I would also like to express my appreciation for your strong and steady support to ...
6) I would like to thank you for attending this blessed event today!
7) It's always a pleasure to host ...
8) Laura and I are proud to have you here for our dinner party.
9) Mr. President, and Mrs. Bush, distinguished guests, ladies and gentlemen, dear friends: First of all, I wish to express on behalf of ... and in my own way, my sincere thanks to you, Mr. President, and Mrs. Bush for your thoughtful arrangements and gracious hospitality.
10) Mr. President, I'm pleased to offer a toast to you and to your gracious wife, and to the people of China.

4.8 COMMUNICATION LABORATORY

A. Give a brief answer to the following questions.
   (1) What is the main purpose of a toast?
   (2) How to write a piece of successful toast?

B. Case Study
   (1) Write a toast delivered by the president to his employees at the end of the year party.
   (2) Prepare a toast for the retirement of your most respected teacher.
   (3) Prepare the best man toast speech or the maid of honor toast speech at Laura Audra's wedding party.
   (4) Write a toast speech at the 30th wedding anniversary of your parents.
   (5) Read the following toast and answer the questions.
      1) On what occasion is this toast delivered?
      2) Who is the addresser of this toast?
      3) What is the addresser of this toast most interested in?
      4) Do you think this toast has realized its purpose? Try to analyze it in detail.

A Toast Delivered at a Press Conference

Mr. Dalton Yap, President of the Chinese Benevolent Association, and Mrs. Yap,
Friends from the CBA,
Leaders of the Chinese Cultural Association and the Chinese Freemason Society,
Fellow Chinese,
Ladies and gentlemen,

It is a great pleasure for my wife and myself to attend tonight's reception hosted by the Chinese Benevolent Association to celebrate the 56th anniversary of the founding of the People's Republic of China. First of all, please allow me to extend, on behalf of the Chinese Government, the festive greetings to all of you, and through you, to the Jamaican Chinese Community.

Born just a few years earlier than the founding of the People's Republic, I am an eyewitness of the great changes having taken place in our motherland in the past 56 years, especially the past 27 years after China started the reform and opening-up. Looking back at the road our motherland has traversed over these 56 years, I am full of strong feeling of pride and dignity. And I believe that the same feeling is shared by our fellow Chinese on such an occasion to celebrate and to remember.

As the Chinese Ambassador to Jamaica, I am extremely happy to see the sound development of bilateral relations between China and Jamaica in recent years, especially this year. The two countries are enjoying the relationship better than ever in the history, we have been expanding our exchanges and cooperation in many fields such as trade, culture, education, media, science and technology, tourism and sports. The highlight of this relationship is the exchange of high-level visits between the two countries, that is, China's Vice President Zeng Qinghong's visit to Jamaica in February and Prime Minister Patterson's visit to China in June. Here I want to mention the Chinese Community's involvement in these important events. CBA has actively participated in the preparation of the first ministerial conference of the China Caribbean Economic and Trade Cooperation Forum which was held in Kingston during Vice President Zeng Qinghong's visit to Jamaica. For Prime Minister Patterson's visit to China, representatives of the Chinese Community were specially selected as members of his delegation, with President Dalton Yap as one of them. The excellent relationship between China and Jamaica all these years has culminated in the establishment of the Jamaican Embassy in China this July. As President Hu Jintao has rightly put it when meeting with Prime Minister Patterson last June in Beijing: "The year 2005 is the year of Sino-Jamaican friendship".

When I am talking about the great achievements China has made and the all-round development of Sino-Jamaican relations, I must express deep appreciation to the Chinese Jamaicans for the contributions they have made to the promotion of relations between their motherland and the country their ancestors chose to live.

Having settled down on this land of wood and water, those pioneers worked very hard and gradually integrated themselves with other ethnic groups in this highly diversified society. The Chinese community now has won high respect from both the Jamaican Government and their fellow Jamaicans for their active participation in the nation building of Jamaica as well as for the fine traditions they have inherited from their ancestors.

Among all these traditions, a precious one is the affection for the culture from their motherland. Although some of you are already the third or fourth generation immigrants here in Jamaica, you still keep a strong feeling towards China and the Chinese culture. I am glad to see the traditional Chinese life style and customs still well preserved in the Chinese Community of Jamaica. Invited by the CBA, some young diplomats of my Embassy are teaching the Chinese course at weekends. They have told me that many times they have almost been moved to tears by the genuine passion and attachment their students hold to the Chinese language, the language once spoken by their ancestors.

The Chinese language is the prime essence and the most important carrier of the Chinese culture. My Embassy will continue to offer help to the CBA's Chinese course and other programmes set up by the Association because they are conducive to carrying forward the traditional Chinese cultural heritage in the Chinese community and, in the end, to the further promotion of Sino-Jamaican relations.

I would also like to express my appreciation for your strong and steady support to the peaceful reunification of our motherland. Immediately after the *Anti Secession Law* was passed by the National People's Congress of China last March, the Chinese Benevolent Association issued a statement to express its resolute and unshakeable support to this law, reaffirming its consistent stand of adhering to the one China policy. This has proved that the early complete reunification of the motherland is the expectation of the Chinese people all over the world. It is my belief that, with such strong support, China's complete unification will definitely be achieved.

The Chinese Community is also an important force in pushing forward the people-to-people exchanges between China and Jamaica. Thanks to the collaboration of the CBA, the performance tours of China's Yangzhou Puppet Theatre and Zunyi Acrobatic Troup in Jamaica turned out to be great successes. Now I have the pleasure to tell you that around May next year, the China National Song and Dance Ensemble will send a troupe to perform in Jamaica. With the support of the CBA and the whole Chinese community in Jamaica, we expect more and more active exchanges in this regard.

Dear friends, the ever-growing relationship between China and Jamaica will provide new opportunities for the cooperation of our two countries. This, I believe, will also bring to our fellow Chinese the fortunate time for your own business.

Now, I'd like to propose a toast to the prosperity of our great motherland and the well-being of the Chinese people, to the continuous development of Sino-Jamaican relations, to the prosperity of the Chinese Community in Jamaica. Cheers!

Unit 5　Minutes

Meeting minutes, like meeting notes, are generally referred to as the brief but accurate records of a formal or informal meeting. But compared with meeting notes, minutes are more formal and they serve as a written record to be kept for future reference and are often required by organizational bylaws. Business talks, discussions, negotiations and so on are generally conducted in different forms of meetings and business meetings may be conducted formally or informally, depending on the company and circumstances, so meeting minutes are supposed to be taken accordingly.

We generally agree that at a meeting, both the organizer and participants of a meeting will intend to go somewhere and endeavor to accomplish something. We often attribute an inefficient meeting to either a weak chair or poor minutes. When our meeting minutes aren't effective, we waste the time we spent in meetings. Without good meeting minutes, we may not remember or recognize:

- What we decided in the meeting;
- What we accomplished in the meeting;
- What we agreed to in terms of next steps (action items).

And when we cannot remember the above items, we end up going in different directions and then meeting again for the same original purpose.

To avoid wasting your time spent in meetings, be sure your minutes answer these questions:

- When was the meeting?
- Who attended?
- Who did not attend? (Include this information if it matters)
- What topics were discussed?
- What was decided?
- What actions were agreed upon?
- Who was to complete the actions? By when?
- Were materials distributed at the meeting? If so, are copies or a link available?
- Is there anything special the reader of the minutes should know or do?
- Is a follow-up meeting scheduled? If so, when, where and why?

According to the degree of the formality of meetings, we usually classify meeting minutes into two types, namely, informal and formal meeting minutes.

When a meeting is held on a quite informal occasion, its minutes can be quite informal, too. Informal minutes usually cover a comprehensive summary, and the minutes taker, in his minutes writing, jogs down or takes down, one after another, the important events of the meeting such as motions, major proposals, plans and resolutions.

Formal minutes are those that usually follow parliamentary procedure, more than often they focus on the specific actions taken at the meeting, including committee reports heard and accepted and motions made and passed.

5.1 THE LAYOUT OF MEETING MINUTES

The layout or template for minutes varies considerably due to the different degrees of formality of the meetings. Furthermore, different companies or organizations may design the layout, if there is any, in different manners. But minutes do need headings so readers can skim for the information they need. The layout or the template should mainly include the following:

- ***Chair***: the name of the person or the group presiding over the meeting;
- ***Date and Time***: the date on which the meeting held and the beginning and ending time of the meeting;
- ***Participants***: the people who attend the meeting;
- ***Topics***: problems presented, talked about, discussed and solved at the meeting;
- ***Decisions***: agreements reached or steps taken;
- ***Actions Agreed Upon***: what has been agreed upon at the meeting;
- ***Person Responsible***: who is held responsible for actions;
- ***Next Meeting***: date and time, location, agenda items, etc.

5.2 DO'S AND DON'TS IN MEETING MINUTES WRITING

* Do write minutes soon after the meeting—preferably within 48 hours. That way, those who attended can be reminded of action items, and those who did not attend will promptly know what happened.
* Don't skip writing minutes just because everyone attended the meeting and knows what happened. Meeting notes serve as a record of the meeting long after people forget what happened.

Format 1

Meeting Minutes for the ABC Company
Chair:
Date and Time:
Participants:
Topics:
Decisions:
Person Responsible:
Next Meeting:
Minutes Taker:

Format 2

Name of Organization:
Purpose of Meeting:
Date/Time:
Chair:

Topic	Discussion	Action	Person Responsible
1			
2			
3			

* Don't describe all the "he said, she said" details unless those details are very important. Record topics discussed, decisions made, and action items.
* Don't include any information that will embarrass anyone (for example, "Then Johnson left the room in anguish or in tears.").
* Do use positive language. Rather than describing the discussion as *heated* or *angry*, use *passionate*, *lively*, or *energetic*—all of which are just as true as the negative words.

5.3 SAMPLE MINUTES

Sample 5 (1)

May 10, 2021

Meeting of the Sales Department

The Sales Department met at 10:00 a.m. on May 10 in Room 512 to discuss the feasibility of a marketing forum to be hosted by the company in about two months' time. Present were Alex Fang, manager of the Sales Department, John Wong, deputy manager of the Sales Department, all the other staff, as well as Alan Smith, deputy general manager of the company in charge of marketing.

　　Mr. Fang highlighted the necessity and importance of the proposed forum, as our company is facing big challenges and the present marketing competition is getting tougher.

　　His opening statement was followed by a lively discussion from all the participants of the meeting. It was agreed that a detailed forum schedule should be drafted and submitted to the company for approval.

　　All participants agreed with the proposal that a marketing forum be hosted by the company and the meeting adjourned at 11:00 a.m.

Jane Wang
Minutes taker

Sample 5 (2)

Minutes of a Monthly Meeting of the Sales Department

Time: 2:00 p.m., May 25, 2021

Venue: Room 512, fifth floor, Sunshine Import & Export Company

Participants: All the staff of the Sales Department

Chair: Alex Fang, manager of the department

Minutes taker: Jane

The main agenda of the meeting:

　　After the meeting was declared open, Alex Fang read the signed letter of approval from the company. In the letter the company authorities gave their official consent to our proposal that a marketing forum be held in our company.

　　The members of the organizing committee of the forum were nominated and chosen.

　　Some suggested holding a press conference to publicize the forthcoming forum, which was agreed unanimously.

　　Discussions were held to decide on the participants to be invited and on the total number of the participants.

　　A detailed schedule was discussed and made at the meeting.

　　The meeting adjourned at 5:00 p.m.

Sample Minutes 5 (3)

Minutes of the Committee on Culture, Media and Sports

January 17, 2021

　　The regular monthly meeting of the Committee on Culture, Media and Sports of the municipality was held in Room 205 of the City Hall at 9:00 a.m. January 17, 2021. The meeting was called to order and presided over by Mr. John Whitehead, Chairman.

　　Proposals

　　The draft report proposed by the chair was brought up, read and approved.

　　Treasurer's Report

Philip Davies reported receipts of $50,000 and expenditures of $25,000 last month. The report was read and accepted.

Resolution

A resolution was adopted unanimously by the Committee on Culture, Media and Sports. Whereas, a Cultural Exchange Forum between our city and our Chinese sister city will be held next month. An Organizing Committee of the forum will be established by this week and Mr. John Whitehead will chair the Organizing Committee. A copy of this resolution will be included in the local newspapers and television stations.

The meeting was adjourned at 11:30 a.m.

Maria Smith
Minutes taker

Sample Minutes 5 (4)

Committee of Maple Leaf Community

Minutes of Meeting

May 17, 2021

The regular quarterly meeting of the Committee Maple Leaf Community was held at Rose Lodge, 2:00 p.m., May 17, 2021. The meeting was called to order and presided by Dr. Roy Brown, Chairman.

Minutes

The minutes of the last meeting were read, discussed and approved.

Treasurer's Report

Philip Davies, treasurer, reported receipts of $5,000 and expenditures of $2,000 since the last meeting, for a current balance of $21,000. The financial report of the committee was read and accepted.

Department Reports

Louise White presented the report of the Social Department. As scheduled, a charity concert by the community will be held in the community park on June 2.

The report of the Improvements Department was presented by Jane Black, who distributed the findings of a survey on the use of community sports facilities.

The meeting was adjourned at 3:30 p.m.

Tina Wong
Minutes taker

5.4 NOTES

(1) chair　主持
(2) chairperson　主席,主持人
(3) attribute ... to ...　将……归咎于……
(4) refer ... to ...　把……归诸;把……提交;使向……请教

(5) accordingly 相应地,因此
(6) accomplish 完成(任务),达到(目的)
(7) a follow-up meeting 续会
(8) jog down (草草地)记录
(9) motion 提议,动议
(10) resolution 决议
(11) unanimously 一致地
(12) feasibility 可行性
(13) highlight 着重,强调
(14) draft 起草
(15) submit 呈送
(16) adjourn 结束;推迟;休(会);推迟考虑(问题等)
(17) agenda (会议)议程

5.5 COMMUNICATION LABORATORY

A. Give a brief answer to the following questions.
(1) What are the major purposes of meeting minutes?
(2) What are the essential elements in minutes writing?
(3) What are the differences between essay writing and minutes writing?
(4) What is the writing style you should adopt in meeting minutes?

B. Case Study
(1) A meeting about the feedback of the quality of your company's products is being held. Supposing you are the minutes taker, please write a copy of an informal meeting minutes of the meeting. You are reminded to include the essential elements of meeting minutes.
(2) A meeting of the Board of Directors about the future marketing strategies of your company is being held. Write a copy of formal meeting minutes.

Unit 6 Itineraries

Literally, an itinerary is a plan or list of the places people will visit on a journey. A journey can be started purely for the appreciation of natural sceneries or sites of historical interest, as well as for shopping in the downtown areas of the cities where these natural sceneries or places of historical interest are located. It can also be arranged for a business trip to several places attending different sessions of meetings based on a given subject. Therefore, the plan can be made either by the person who is engaged in the journey or by a travel agency or an organization which promotes the journey.

Itineraries drawn for sight seeing tell people the whole range of their activities on their journey. They help organize the time and places for people to start for their destinations as well as the time and places where people gather to leave for home, the means for people to travel, the hotels for people to stay over nights, the restaurants for people to have dinners at, and the sites for people to enjoy and buy souvenirs. They sometimes offer different routes to meet the preference of different travelers. Itineraries of this kind drawn by travel agencies are often used to advertise travel services. They are made to arrange different activities along different travel routes for tourists who prefer group traveling to individual trips. Drawn by individuals for their own use, itineraries can help individual travelers to sort out what will happen on their way to predestined destinations, hence greatly facilitating their journeys.

If it is an itinerary about a business or academic conference held in sessions in a certain place or sometimes more than one place, it normally informs people of registration time and place, hotels for staying conventioneers, places for opening and concluding ceremony, places for different sessions of the meeting, restaurants for meals, recreational sites near the meeting sites, prospecting topics for next conference, as well as time and plan for next conference, time and places where the conventioneers are to take souvenir pictures, time and place for departure, etc. Sometimes, the host of the conference will organize tours around the meeting sites for conventioneers, who are to decide to go or not. When this happens, the itinerary will also include information of this kind. Itineraries of conference journey are frequently used to arrange large-scale meetings with conventioneers from various places. They are especially useful in organizing the different sessions of the meeting. By resorting to conference itineraries, conventioneers are able to locate the meeting time and place.

A sight-seeing journey or a conference-attending journey usually lasts a couple of days. Of course, there will be journeys which last only one day. There will also be journeys that last weeks or even at least a whole month. However long a journey may cover, itineraries are just plans about what people will do at given time in given places over a period of time.

6.1 THE LAYOUT OF ITINERARIES

Being a plan about people's different actions around a given theme at different periods of time in different places, an itinerary can be conveyed in the format of table listing different information in different grids under different subjects. A text version of the same itinerary can also be rendered providing that information belonging to the same group is presented in paragraphs under the same headline.

With regard to the different purposes and planners of an itinerary, there are some other ways to present it. If it is an itinerary drawn by a travel agency, it can take the format of a brochure advertising the special services that travel agency can offer.

With the ready access to the Internet almost everywhere, many travel agencies are now providing customized itineraries to their clients through their online service. Prospective clients can choose their convenient time and favored destinations or routes on the websites powered by such travel agencies. Then, they will get an itinerary meeting their individual demands. In this case, the itinerary takes the format of web pages.

Since itineraries can be used to draw a plan for a conference journey, they border on another two forms of business writing, namely agenda and schedule. An agenda is a list of things to be discussed at a meeting of a group, whereas a schedule refers to phases of an action with corresponding approximate dates. In itineraries concerning business trips about conferences, detailed information will be offered about the list of things to be discussed at different sessions of a meeting. Different sessions of the meeting held at different time that cover from several hours to several weeks are in fact different phases of the meeting. For these two reasons, an itinerary can also be realized in the format of agendas and schedules. In most cases, the format of an itinerary concerning conferences just merges with that of an agenda or a schedule. Itineraries concerning conferences can also be personalized online at the websites of those organizations who host conferences.

No matter what forms it may take, an itinerary usually should include the following information:

- What event(s) will take place?
- When will the event(s) take place?
- Where will the event(s) take place?
- Who will take part in the event(s)?
- Who is responsible for the formulation of the itinerary?

- Who will organize the event(s)?

In one word, an itinerary usually consists of four basic elements: time, places, individuals (or organizations) and events. These four elements should be positioned as is shown in the following examples.

Format 1

The Baltimore Mill Hotel and Restaurant	
Introduction	1
Time and Means of Getting Here	3
Activities Arranged for Visitors	5
Accommodation	12
The Restaurant at Bellows Mill	19
Further Information	21

This is an itinerary presented in the format of brochure by a travel agency. Different items of the itinerary are to be presented in details part by part after the tale of contents.

Format 2

Tasmania Island of Inspiration
The following suggested itinerary helps you locate some of our most exciting wildlife experiences. See little penguins, colonies of Australian fur seals, regal white-bellied sea eagles, shy echidnas, nocturnal quolls, devils, wallabies and wombats.
DAY 1—Launceston to St Helens
DAY 2—St Helens to Bicheno
DAY 3—Bicheno to Port Arthur
DAY 4—Port Arthur
DAY 5—Port Arthur to Hobart, Launceston or Devonport

This is an itinerary presented in the text version by a travel agency in promoting its business. Emphasis is laid upon different phases of the journey organized in terms of different days.

Format 3

University of St Andrews Visiting Day Itinerary
Name: Miss A. N. Other
09:15   Registration
Lower College Hall, St Salvator's Quadrangle
09:45   University Walking Tour
Leaving from Lower College Hall, St Salvator's Quadrangle (Tour ends with a visit to a Hall of

Residence)

10:45 Sports Centre
   University Sports Centre, North Haugh
12:10 Graduate Careers Talk
   Buchanan Lecture Theatre, Buchanan Building, Union Street
13:30 Welcome Talk / University Overview
   School 3, St Salvator's Quadrangle
14:15 Meeting I
   First Academic Departmental Appointment
15:15 Meeting II
   Second Academic Departmental Appointment

This is a personalized itinerary made online for the drafter's own convenience. Different events that constitute the whole journey are organized in time units. It is presented in the format of web page at the following website: http://www.st-andrews.ac.uk/admissions/VisitingtheUniversity/Personalitinerary/.

Format 4

United Nations Economic and Social Commission for Asia and the Pacific

Itinerary for March, 2004
Terry Smith, General Secretary of Economic Cooperation Department

Date	Headline
26/March/2004	The United Nations Secretary-General's message on World Health Day, 7 April 2004
26/March/2004	Regional Policy Dialogue on WTO issues in a Post-Cancun Trading Environment
24/March/2004	UN organizes Seminar on Implications of the "Bangkok Agreement" for prospective member countries
24/March/2004	The United Nations Secretary-General's message on International Day of Solidarity with Detained and Missing Staff Members, 25 March 2004

This is a business itinerary presented in the format of tables. Different types of information are organized in terms of time and subject.

Unlike notices or letters of application, the forms of an itinerary are very flexible.

6.2 THE PLANNING OF ITINERARIES

Careful planning is indispensable to an effective itinerary. Before starting to write an itinerary, the drafter should organize all the information into recognizable parts, which will enable the reader to learn about the four elements of an itinerary immediately. An itinerary customarily comprises three parts:

The Heading. The heading part usually outlines the purpose of the itinerary. If it is one predominantly about traveling, the heading may tell what kinds of wonderful journeys people may have. It can also be something about a travel agency, a hotel, or a site of interest which promises people wonderful traveling experience. If it is one about conference, it generally tells people about the subject of the conference.

The Drafter. The Drafter of an itinerary refers to the person or the organization that is responsible for the formulation of it. More often than not, the date on which the itinerary is released is to be put immediately below the drafter. Sometimes, the drafter of an itinerary can be omitted when it is a personal itinerary or when the organization which has prepared can be inferred either from the heading or from the body part of it.

The Body. The body part of an itinerary may vary from one to another. If it is in the form of a table, the information will be organized in terms of the four elements of time, places, persons, and events. If it is presented in the form of a text, the information will be organized according to the division of time, or different phases of the whole event. In itineraries about a conference, the body part of different phases of a conference may take all the parts of an agenda, namely the heading, the date, the time, the venue, and lists of topics to be discussed. It may also take the parts of a schedule: activity, start time, and completion.

After the organization of different sorts of information into different parts, the drafter should then go on to plan about the form the itinerary is going to take. Whatever form, the itinerary should meet its purpose in directing people about what is to happen at given time in future.

The general plan for an instructive itinerary is as follows. The heading outlines its purpose, the drafter indicates the person responsible for the organization of a series of events, and the body details the schedule for the series of events.

6.3 THE TONE OF ITINERARIES

Tone refers to the drafter's voice. Being a plan to guide people about what to do, when and where to do it, the itinerary should be conveyed in such a tone as to make the reader of it clear about their responsibility and ready to carry it out. Therefore, the tone of an itinerary can range from objective to subjective.

The tone of an itinerary is determined by its writing purpose. In business itineraries about conference, the tone used in presenting the arrangement of different events should be as objective and factual as possible. In a business itinerary offered by a travel agency to promote its business, all the information should be listed in an subjective tone that sounds as persuasive as possible.

6.4 PRESENTATION OF ITINERARIES

In presenting the contents of an itinerary, the drafter should adhere to the following principles.

(1) Consistent in Format

An itinerary should be presented in the same style throughout. A mixture of different forms may lead to confusion on the part of the reader. It is especially true of the body part of an itinerary. The format of texts shall not be used together with the format of tables.

(2) Sparing No Information

In writing an itinerary, the drafter should leave out no relevant information. The incompleteness in information will also lead a sense of confusion on the part of the reader.

(3) Logic in Arrangement

Logically arranged events of a journey or a conference in an itinerary will bring both efficiency and success to the promoter of the journey or the host of the conference. On the other hand, they will enable a successful understanding of the itinerary in the reader. Illogically organized itineraries always lead to great confusion in the reader and consequently great difficulty in carrying them out.

(4) Explicit in Statement

An itinerary should be clear in its purpose and arrangement. Involved sentence structures and difficult words often lead to difficulty in understanding. Every element in an itinerary should be made distinct. To do this, some part of the itinerary should be printed in bold letters or in capital forms.

Try to make the itinerary text more reader-friendly by applying some of the highlighting techniques: fonts, headings, white space, charts, graphs, pictures, bolded words, bullets and graphics.

6.5 EFFECTIVE ITINERARY CHECKLIST

The following is a list of points to check when you write an effective itinerary:
- Have you used the correct itinerary format that is most effective in realizing its purpose?
- Will the person who reads the itinerary be able to understand the message?
- Have you included all relevant information?

- Is your writing style concise and explicit?
- Have you achieved the correct tone?
- Is your page layout reader-friendly? Have you used highlighting techniques for accessibility?
- Is your organization of the information logical?
- Have you checked spelling, grammar and punctuation?

6.6 SAMPLE ITINERARIES

Sample 6 (1): Example of a Local Business Itinerary

Bellows Mill Hotel and Restaurant

Introduction

Only 30 miles north of London and you will escape the hustle and bustle of city life for a complete change of scenery. At Bellows Mill you can relax in the tranquil surroundings of 21 acres of lakes and woodland.

How Would You Get Here?

Leave your car behind and arrive at Tring Station from Euston. Trains run every 20 minutes.

From there we will collect you by car and 10 minutes later you will arrive at Bellows Mill.

If you travel by car it will take approximately 1 hour from central London.

What Will You Do Here?

You have a variety of activities to choose from to while away the hours and you can be as idle or energetic as you like.

Those wishing to be more active can hire electric bicycles, visit nearby places of interest and exercise their brain power with our treasure hunt around the picturesque local villages. You can also play tennis (rackets and balls supplied), or go gliding at the nearby London gliding club. You might like to cycle to and around Whipsnade Zoo which is just 1 mile away, albeit it up a very steep hill.

Those prepared to travel a little further afield may like to explore Woburn, 10 miles from Bellows Mill. The town itself has some fascinating shops and places to eat, with a Farmers' Market on the third Sunday of every month, 11 a.m. – 3 p.m. Woburn Abbey is a magnificent country house with stunning grounds.

There are many lovely places in the vicinity if you enjoy walking. For example, Ashridge Forest, which is not to be missed, especially when the bluebells are out. Also there's Ivinghoe Beacon, part of the Ridgeway walk, and on the doorstep, the Totternhoe Knolls.

For bird lovers The Lodge at Sandy is an easy 40 minute drive, and Tring Reservoir is

7 miles. There are many bird species to be seen at Bellows Mill, including kingfishers. In Tring, there is an antiques auction every alternate Saturday and the Walter Rothschild Zoological Museum is a good standby when the weather is bad. Bletchley Park is a 30-minute drive.

The beautifully restored Rex Cinema at Berkhamsted has an excellent program which includes foreign language and art house films as well as all the box office hits. The seats are luxurious and you can even book a private table with champagne if you are celebrating a special occasion. Advance booking for any film is essential.

Local theatres include The Old Town Hall, Hemel Hempstead, 15 minutes, The Stables, Wavendon, 25 minutes and Milton Keynes Theatre, 30 minutes, all of which are easy to get to with free, convenient parking.

Accommodation

The rooms at Bellows Mill have comfortable beds, with en suite bathrooms and TVs. There is also a self catering option, "Mill End", which can accommodate 5 guests. Mill End Garden is surrounded by a little stream, which is the county boundary of Bedfordshire and Buckinghamshire.

Meals—The Restaurant at Bellows Mill

The restaurant, which is open to non-residents, serves Fairtrade tea and coffee, and uses local produce and serves seasonal food wherever possible. The eggs are free range from the neighbouring farm.

Hampers can be ordered in advance, if you would like a picnic lunch, or you can have a Barbecue on the patio. Ingredients will be provided. Sample menus can be found on our website.

Further Information

For further details please see our website www.bellowsmill.co.uk

Sample 6 (2): An Itinerary Drafted by a Travel Agency

Tasmania, Island of Inspiration
The Devil You Don't Know

Discover amazing wildlife in Tasmania's parks, forests, seas and skies.

Have you ever wanted to see nocturnal activities of the Tasmanian devil? Glimpse a timid duck-billed platypus or learn the truth and tragedy of the Tasmanian tiger?

The following suggested itinerary helps you locate some of our most exciting wildlife experiences. See little penguins, colonies of Australian fur seals, regal white-bellied sea eagles, shy echidnas, nocturnal quolls, devils, wallabies and wombats.

DAY 1—Launceston to St Helens

En route from Launceston to the East Coast (B81), take time out in Scottsdale to view quolls, echidnas, bettongs, platypuses, kangaroos and <u>wallabies</u> in the wild on a <u>four-wheel-drive tour of the north-east</u>. The seaside town of St Helens (A3) is the gateway to

Mt William National Park, a remote and exquisitely beautiful region in the far northeast of the State. Large Forester kangaroos feed in the grasslands. This national park now protects the largest surviving population of Foresters, savagely culled by European settlers in the 19th century when clearing land for pasture. Joeys are in the pouch from late summer until early October.

Mt William is also a great place for dusk wombat-viewing, is home to approximately 100 bird species, and is a landfall for many Bass Strait migratory birds. Yellow-tailed black cockatoos and introduced kookaburras are sure to catch your attention with their noisy calls.

OVERNIGHT SUGGESTION: St Helens

DAY 2—St Helens to Bicheno

Bicheno, an attractive seaside town on the East Coast Escape touring route (A3), with lots of opportunities to get close to nature.

Near Bicheno you can see Tasmanian devils, wombats and kangaroos and other fascinating mammals, birds and reptiles—some native, some not.

See dainty little penguins on a one-hour sunset tour. Alternatively, marvel at the wonderful marine life beneath the transparent hull of your vessel as it glides through the clear, sheltered waters of Bicheno's marine park and gulch. The trip lasts 45 minutes. Scuba-diving in the close-by marine reserve is also an option, to see seahorses and weedy dragons.

Bicheno and Coles Bay are both great bases for visiting the dazzling beaches and pink granite mountains of Freycinet National Park. The walk to Wineglass Bay is one of Tasmania's most scenic, but a marine wildlife cruise gives you an entirely different perspective on the beauty of this area. Dolphins may follow in your wake, Australian fur seals may perform for you, and if you are especially lucky, humpback and southern right whales may cross your path on their annual spring migration.

OVERNIGHT SUGGESTION: Bicheno or Coles Bay

DAY 3—Bicheno to Port Arthur

An optional day trip to Maria Island National Park is always memorable. Set aside a full day, as this is an excellent place for snorkelling, scuba diving (bring your own equipment), bird watching, rock-pool rambling and walking amid stunning scenery. Daily passenger ferries to the island depart from Triabunna and the Eastcoaster Resort at Louisville.

Maria Island is a haven for migratory birds and wildlife. Tasmanian native hens, Cape Barren geese, Forester kangaroos and Bennetts wallabies browse throughout the day on the plains surrounding the historic convict settlement of Darlington. Tasmanian pademelons abound, and eastern barred bandicoots can often be seen in the moonlight if you choose to camp on the island overnight. In the evocative words of Lonely Planet's *Watching Wildlife Australia*, "Ponds around the old convict settlement reverberate with the plunk of eastern banjo frogs and the distinctive call (ree-ree-ree-ree) of the brown tree frog."

Back on mainland Tasmania, follow the coastline south (C320) to the Tasman Peninsula along to the Convict Trail touring route (A9). Sweeping beaches, grand, wave-sculptured rock formations such as the Blowhole and Remarkable Cave and the curious fractured charm of the Tessellated Pavement are among the Peninsula's many natural attractions. Both wedge-tailed eagles and white-bellied sea eagles are regularly seen. The grim history of convict life at Port Arthur Historic Site, Australia's pre-eminent historic penal settlement, draws visitors from around the world to this stunning part of Tasmania.

Visibility in these temperate diving waters is so high that *National Geographic* magazine's top dive photographer, David Doubilet, has described Tasmania as having the most "accessible underwater wilderness in the world". Cliffs that tower above the surface descend dramatically to the ocean floor, creating canyons and caves amid huge forests of giant kelp up to 30 meters (100 feet) high, home to sea dragons, handfish and seals. Take one of the options offered by local dive tour operators who have an intimate knowledge of the area and all the equipment you need.

Cruise the waters of the Tasman Peninsula and around Tasman Island, and view Australia's highest sea cliffs, majestic sea eagles and other varieties of sea birds. See hundreds of Australian fur seals and occasionally leopard and elephant seals. Perhaps be shadowed by a wandering albatross, the world's largest flying bird.

OVERNIGHT SUGGESTION: Port Arthur

DAY 4—Port Arthur

Today choose between bird-watching or viewing devils, golden possums, white-bellied sea eagles and a host of other fascinating wildlife the local wildlife park at Taranna. Consider spending an extra night on the Tasman Peninsula to experience all its history and beauty.

DAY 5—Port Arthur to Hobart, Launceston or Devonport

Return to Hobart, Launceston or Devonport to catch your flight or the Spirit of Tasmania back to mainland Australia.

Sample 6 (3): A Conference Itinerary

Manitoba Trade and Investment

Business Delegate's Itinerary/Program
Business Mission to India Led by Manitoba Premier Gary Doer
New Delhi, Mumbai and Chandigarh
February 13 – 17, 2006

Sunday, February 12, 2006 NEW DELHI and CHANDIGARH		
	NEW DELHI PROGRAM	**CHANDIGARH PROGRAM**
8:00 p.m.	Dinner with invited guests	
Monday, February 13, 2006 CHANDIGARH / NEW DELHI		
	NEW DELHI PROGRAM	**CHANDIGARH PROGRAM**
9:00 – 11:00 a.m.	Open for Individual meeting programs Taj Mahal, Longchamp	9:00 – 10:00 a.m. **Chandigarh Market Briefing** The Taj Chandigarh Hotel Ballroom
11:30 a.m.		Reception with Confederation of Indian Industry-CII
The Taj Mahal Hotel Number One, Mansingh Road New Delhi 110011		
Tel: 011 – 91 – 11 – 5551 – 3607 **Fax:** 011 – 91 – 11 – 5551 – 369		
16:00 p.m. – 6:30 p.m.	New Delhi Market Briefing	**The Taj Mahal Hotel Longchamp**
Tuesday, February 14, 2006 NEW DELHI		
7:30 – 8:30 a.m.	**Breakfast meeting**	**Taj Mahal Hotel**
10:00 a.m. – 12:00 p.m.	**New Delhi Business Program** One-to-one meetings	**Taj Mahal Hotel**
2:30 **p.m.**	**Registration/Reception**	**Taj Mahal Hotel** Diwan-I-Am Room
12:45 – 2:00 p.m.	**Luncheon**	
Afternoon	**Individual Business Program**	**Taj Mahal Hotel**
7:00 – 8:30 p.m.	**Manitoba Reception** Sponsored by Jorgenson Group of Companies	**Taj Mahal Hotel** Poolside Lawns
Wednesday, February 15, 2006 MUMBAI		

(continuous)

Taj Mahal Palace and Tower		
Apollo Bunder, Mumbai 400 001		
Tel: 011-91-22-5665-3366		
Fax: 011-91-22-5664-0323/24		
3:30-5:00 p.m.	Mumbai Market Briefing	Taj Mahal Palace Gateway Hall
7:00-10:00 p.m.	Reception/Dinner Hosted by Scotiabank	Taj Mahal Palace Gateway Hall
Official Program Ends		

Sample 6 (4): A Personal Meeting Itinerary

Personal Meeting Itinerary
2019 Fall Meeting
Professor Smith, Sate University of California

Monday Morning			
Time	Session	Location	Title
8:30		MCC2001	Opening **Presiding**: A L Gordon, Lamont-Doherty Earth Observatory; W Kuhnt, Institute for Geosciences, University of Kiel
10:20	PP12B	MCC3001	Climate Impacts of Changes to the Thermohaline Circulation I (joint with A, OS, GC) **Presiding**: J Chiang, University of California; C Morrill, National Center for Atmospheric Research
Monday Afternoon			
Time	Session	Location	Title
13:40	OS13A	MCC3012	Present and Past Indonesian Throughflow Variability: PAGES-IMAGES I (joint with PP, GC) **Presiding**: A L Gordon, Lamont-Doherty Earth Observatory; W Kuhnt, Institute for Geosciences, University of Kiel

(continuous)

Time	Session	Location	Title
13:40	OS13A-01	MCC3012	Observed Variability in the Indonesian Throughflow: A Review * J Sprintall INVITED
16:00	PP14A	Marriott Salon 8	Emiliani Lecture: On Glaciations and Their Causes (joint with A, OS, GC) **Presiding**: D W Lea, Department of Geological Sciences, University of California, Santa Barbara; B Otto-Bliesner, National Center for Atmospheric Research
16:05	PP14A-01	Marriot Salon 8	Emiliani Lecture: On Glaciations and their Causes * M E Raymo INVITED
Tuesday Morning			
Time	Session	Location	Title
8:00	OS21D	MCC3012	Ocean Sciences: Discoveries From Space I (joint with A, B, C, GC) **Presiding**: K A Kelly, University of Washington; L Fu, Jet Propulsion Laboratory, California Institute of Technology
8:00	OS21D-01	MCC3012	Ocean Circulation from Space: An Overview * S T Gille INVITED
8:45	OS21D-04	MCC3012	High-resolution mapping of the Arctic sea ice cover with RADARSAT and ICES at for climate and process studies * R Kwok
10:50	OS22B-03	MCC3012	Concluding Meeting **Presiding**: A L Gordon, Lamont-Doherty Earth Observatory; W Kuhnt, Institute for Geosciences, University of Kiel

6.7 NOTES

1. An agenda normally consists of five parts: heading, date, time, venue, subject, and possible topics to be discussed at the meeting. For example,

China Telecommunication Co, Ltd.
Agenda of the 15th Meeting of
The Third Board of Directors

Date: May 28, 2021
Time: 8:50 – 11:30
Venue: 210 Pearl Hall
Subject: Nominating new members of next board of directors

(1) Nominating committee's changes in presidency of China Telecommunication Co., Ltd.
(2) Nominating committee's changes in secretary of board of directors of China Telecommunication Co., Ltd.
(3) Reforming salary systems
(4) Reforming security systems

The Managing Director's Office
May 25, 2021

2. Generally speaking, schedules are categorized into phases of action with corresponding approximate dates. For example,

The Schedule for Laying Cable Lines
on the New Campus

K. A. Kelly, Project Manager
Southampton Construction Co., Ltd.
February 14, 2021

Activity	Start Date	Completion
Site inspection	4/3/2021	4/10/2021
Site preparation	4/15/2021	4/30/2021
Foundation excavation	5/1/2021	5/12/2021
Pipe laying	5/14/2021	5/28/2021
Cabling	5/14/2021	5/28/2021

3. The Personal Meeting Itinerary will allow you to select the sessions and papers you want to see at the selected meeting. Search through the titles, add or delete items from your schedule. Return at any time to revise your selections. You can also personalize your itinerary, e-mail a copy to yourself, or share it with your colleagues.

6.8 COMMUNICATION LABORATORY

A. Give a brief answer to the following questions.
(1) What are the functions of itineraries?
(2) What are the differences between itineraries drafted by a travel agency and those presented by a conference committee?
(3) What are the relationships between itineraries and agendas?
(4) What factors are to be included in a successful itinerary?

B. Case Study
(1) Write a personal itinerary for honeymoon trip lasting two weeks.
(2) Write an itinerary about your hometown for the local travel agency.
(3) Write an agenda of the board meeting about the election of a new president.
(4) Write a schedule for a graduate thesis.

Unit 7 Forms and Diagrams

Forms and diagrams are two concise and comprehensive types of business communication that visually present important information. Forms are documents with blank spaces to be filled in with particulars before it is executed. Diagrams are drawings intended to explain how something works or to show the relation between the parts. Forms and diagrams are helpful and efficient in business communication as they contain large volumes of information of various categories and systematize collection of littery and immethodical information.

7.1 TYPES OF FORMS

Application Form. An application form is a type of widely used form that requires certain facts to be stated briefly and exactly.

An application form usually includes contents as follows:
- Personal data such as name, sex, native place, marital status, health, contact information;
- Specific requirements on the applied items (a school, a course, a post ...);
- Declaration;
- One's signature, usually hand-written.

Registration Form. A registration form is used widely for various purposes, such as arrival/departure, enrollment, employment, temporary residence.

A registration form usually includes contents as follows:
- Personal data of the one who is to fill out the form, including name, date of birth, occupation, native place, ID number or passport number;
- Cause of registration (e.g. on business trip, for study abroad);
- Contact information;
- Declaration;
- Signature.

Different forms are different in requirements. While designing a form, you should decide on the following items:
- What is your purpose of making this form (for survey, for applicants to fill in ...)?
- Which is the most appropriate format and layout for the form?

- Which items should be included in your form to best serve your purpose?

When filling out a form, you should always note the following:

- Read the directions carefully for correct writing (Print, Block/Capital Letters, Bold Type ...)?
- Supply information that is exactly the truth;
- Write your name in accordance with that in your passport and other official documents;
- State all the information legibly;
- Write date in required sequence;
- If not specified, Americans tend to cross a selection instead of ticking as people in most countries do.

Sample 7 (1)

Visa Application Form

1. Last Name(s) (*List All Spellings*) Wang	2. First Name(s) (*List All Spellings*) Wu	3. Full Name (*in Native Alphabet*) (请填中文全名) 王五
4. Clan or Tribe Name (*If Applicable*)		5. Spouse's Full Name (*If Married*)
6. Father's Full Name Wang Si		7. Mother's Full Name Li Li
8. Full Name and Address of Contact Person or Organization in the United States (*Include Telephone Number*) Sally Peterson Address: 1840 Industrial Drive, Suite 160 Libertyville, Illinois 60048 U.S.A. Tele. No: 001-847-281-9822		
9. List All Countries You have Entered in the Last Ten Years (Give the Year of Each Visit) Canada, 2005		10. Have You Ever Lost a Passport or Had One Stolen? ☐ Yes ☒ No
11. Do You Have Any Specialized Skills or Training, Including Firearms, Explosives, Nuclear, Biological, or Chemical Experience? ☐ Yes ☒ No If YES, please explain.		
12. Have You Ever Performed Military Service? ☐ Yes ☒ No		If Yes, Give Name of Country, Branch of Service, Rank/Position, Military Specialty and Dates of Service.
13. Have You Ever Been in an Armed Conflict, Either as a Participant or Victim? ☐ Yes ☒ No If YES, please explain.		

Sample 7 (2)

Application Form for Foreigners Wishing to Study in China
(Short-term Chinese Course)

Name in Full	Sherry Brian	Nationality		British	Photo
Date of Birth Day - month - year	23 January, 1982	Place of Birth		London, UK	
Marital Status	Married	Sex	Female	Religion	
Permanent Address	20 Great Tower Street, London Post Code: EC3R 5AT					
Tel. No.	020-7023-8488	E-mail		Sb1982@hotmail.com	
Highest Education Level	Bachelor's Degree	Passport No.		P2323	
		Valid until		30 December, 2007	
Employer or Educational Institution	XYZ College	Occupation			Teacher
Do you want to reserve a room (bed) on campus?					Yes ☑ No ☐
Chun Hui yuan-Double Room ¥60/day (approx. USD $8) ☐					
Chun Hui yuan-Single Room ¥80/day (approx. USD $10) ☑					
If the room you applied for is not available	Would like to be arranged an alternative room on campus ☐				
	Would like to rent an apartment by yourself ☑				
Intended Duration	From 1 September, 2006 to 30 October, 2007				
Guarantor in China & Tel	Wu Lilin 025-12132312				
Source of Funding	Scholarship ☐ Self-Supporting ☑ Other ☐				
Will you take elective courses?	Calligraphy ☑ Chinese Painting ☑				
Reasons for Studying in China	I'm interested in Chinese culture and am eager to learn more about this marvelous land.				

I hereby affirm that:
1. All the information in this form is true and correct.
2. I shall abide by the laws of the Chinese Government and the regulations of the School.
Date: 12 D July M 2006 Y

Applicant's Signature

Sherry Brian

Sample 7 (3)

Language Teaching Reform Conference

Registration Form

5th National Language Teaching Reform Conference, 1 - 10 Sept. 2007,

Nanjing, China

Last Name: Green	**First Name**: Erica	**Title**: Professor
University/Organization: ABC University		
Faculty/School/Department: Foreign Languages Department		
Street: Chunshui	**E-mail**: eg000@hotmail.com	
City: Wuxi	**Phone**: 13333333333	
Postcode: 214000	**Country**: China	
Preferred Name for Conference Name Tag: Prof. Erica Green		
Are you presenting a paper at the 2007 Conference? YES ☑ NO ☐		

Completed registration form must be e-mailed to:

ltrc2007@hotmail.com

For detailed information contact:

Mr. Liu Xin

Telephone Number: +86 - 25 - 12345678

Fax: +86 - 25 - 12345678

Sample 7 (4)

Registration Form of Temporary Residence

Type of Certificate	Passport	Certificate No.	P4578
Surname	Green	Given Name	Raymond
Sex	Male	Date of Birth (*dd-month-yyyy*)	2 January, 1985
Nationality	British	Object of Stay	On Business
Where from and to	From London to Shanghai		
Date of Check-in	May 12, 2021	Duration of Stay	15 days
Room No.	1208	Rent	$60 per day
Remarks			

7.2 TYPES OF DIAGRAMS

Pie Chart. A pie chart displays value data as percentages of the whole. Categories are represented by individual slices. The size of the slice is determined by the value. Pie charts are typically used to show percentages.

Sample 7 (5)

As shown in the above sample, employees' educational background of a firm is clearly stated with different slices representing respective percentages.

Bar Chart. A bar chart displays series as sets of horizontal bars that are grouped by category. Values are represented by the length of the bars as measured by the x-axis. Category labels are displayed on the y-axis. Bar charts are typically used to compare values between categories.

Sample 7 (6)

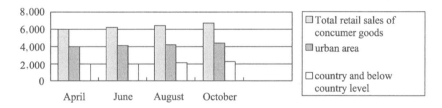

From the above bar chart, we identify the retail sales of consumer goods in different areas, and thus can easily see the difference and make comparison.

Line Chart. A line chart displays series as a set of points connected by a line. Values are represented by the height of the point as measured by the y-axis. Category labels are displayed on the x-axis. Line charts are typically used to compare values over time.

Sample 7 (7)

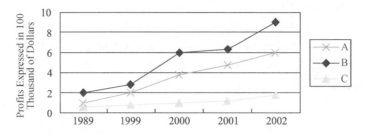

A— the chain stores located in the downtown area
B— the chain stores situated in a densely populated district
C— the chain stores located in the suburbs of the city

In the line chart above, the three curve lines represent respectively a company's profits from 1998 to 2002 in three areas.

Flow Chart. A flow chart, also called flow diagram or flow sheet, is a schematic representation of a sequence of operations, as in a manufacturing process or computer program.

Sample 7 (8)

Performance Evaluation Chart

| Set standards for performance evaluation |

⇩

| Exchange views with employees to be evaluated and decide if adjustment to the standards is necessary |

⇩

| Grade employees' performance in accordance with the standards |

⇩

| Interviewing employees individually |

⇩

| Make improvement by providing employees with necessary training and promotions |

Organization Chart. An organization chart is one that tells the internal structure and composition of a company, an organization ...

Sample 7 (9)

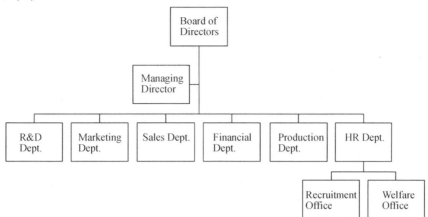

To design a chart for a certain purpose, follow the tips given below:
- Identify your purpose;
- Select the chart (line chart, pie chart ...) that serves your purpose best;
- Decide the data for charts, which usually is organized into three areas: **values**, **category groups**, **and series groups**. The following sample helps you with the understanding of the three items.

Values. When you define a chart, you add at least one value series to the chart. Values determine the size of the chart element for each category group. For example, values determine the height of a column/bar in a bar chart and the size of a slice in a pie chart.

Categories. Use categories to group data. Categories provide the labels for chart elements. For example, in a bar chart, category labels are placed on the x-axis of the chart, one for each set of columns.

Series Groups. Series groups are optional. You can define a series group to add an additional dimension of data to a report. For example, in a column chart that displays sales by product, you can add a series group to display sales by year for each product. Series group labels are placed in the legend of the chart.

Sample 7 (10)

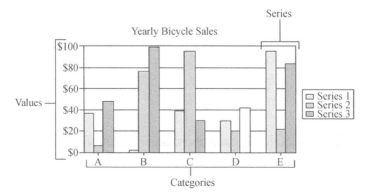

Series groups are dynamic. A chart that uses series groups displays a chart element for each series group for each category.

7.3 NOTES

One of the important skills concerning graphs and diagrams is to interpret. You may find the following words and expressions helpful in making presentations with diagrams.

(1) 上升　increase, rise, ascend, core, surge, go up, climb, mount, level up

(2) 下降　decrease, fall, drop, descend, decline, reduce, lessen, level down

(3) 稳定　stable, steady, remain/maintain/keep/be the same as/similar to fluctuate, fluctuation, rise and fall, up and down

(4) 占　occupy, take up, account for, gain

(5) 而　while, however, whereas, on the other hand, actually / in fact

(6) 相比　by contrast, on the contrary, likewise, compared with

(7) 最高点　the highest, the top, the summit, the peak, the most

(8) 最低点　bottom, less, least, rock bottom

(9) 平均　mean, average

(10) 趋势　tendency, trend, inclination

(11) The table shows the changes in the number of ... over the period from ... to ...
　　该表格描述了在……年和……年之间……数量的变化。

(12) The bar chart illustrates that ...
　　该柱状图展示了……

(13) The graph provides some interesting data regarding ...
　　该图为我们提供了有关……有趣数据。

(14) The diagram shows (that) ...
　　该图向我们展示了……

(15) The pie graph depicts (that) ...
　　该饼形图揭示了……

(16) This is a curve graph which describes the trend of ...
　　这个曲线图描述了……的趋势。

(17) The figures/statistics show (that) ...
　　数据(字)表明……

(18) The tree diagram reveals how ...
　　该树形图向我们揭示了如何……

(19) The data/statistics show (that) ...
　　该数据(字)表明……

(20) The data/statistics/figures lead us to the conclusion that ...
　　这些数据资料令我们得出结论……

(21) As is shown/demonstrated/exhibited in the diagram/graph/chart/table ...
如图所示……

(22) According to the chart/figures ...
根据这些表(数字)……

(23) As is shown in the table ...
如表格所示……

(24) As can be seen from the diagram, great changes have taken place in ...
从图中可以看出……发生了巨大变化。

(25) From the table/chart/diagram/figure, we can see clearly that ... or it is clear/apparent from the chart that ...
从图表我们可以很清楚(明显)看到……

(26) This is a graph which illustrates ...
这个图表向我们展示了……

(27) This table shows the changing proportion of a & b from ... to ...
该表格描述了……年到……年间 a 与 b 的比例关系。

(28) The graph, presented in a pie chart, shows the general trend in ...
该图以饼形图形式描述了……总的趋势。

(29) This is a column chart showing ...
这个柱形图描述了……

(30) As can be seen from the graph, the two curves show the fluctuation of ...
如图所示,两根曲线表明……的波动情况。

(31) Over the period from ... to ... the ... remained level.
在……至……期间……基本不变。

(32) In the year between ... and ...
在……年到……年期间……

(33) In the 3 years spanning from 2018 through 2021 ...
2018 年至 2021 年三年里……

(34) From then on / from this time onwards ...
从那时起……

(35) The number of ... remained steady/stable from (month/year) to (month/year) ...
……月(年)至……月(年)……的数量基本不变。

(36) The percentage of ... stayed the same between ... and ...
……至……期间……的比率维持不变。

(37) The number sharply went up to ...
数字急剧上升至……

(38) The figures peaked at ... in month/year.
……的数目在……月(年)达到顶点,为……

(39) The percentage remained steady at ...
比例维持在……

(40) The percentage of ... is slightly larger/smaller than that of ...
……的比例比……的比例略高(低)。

(41) There is not a great deal of difference between ... and ...
……与……的区别不大。

(42) The graphs show a threefold increase in the number of ...
这些图表表明……的数目增长了三倍。

(43) ... decreased year by year while ... increased steadily.
……逐年减少,而……逐步上升。

(44) The situation reached a peak (a high point at) ... of ... %.
……的情况(局势)到达顶(高)点,为……百分点。

(45) The figures/situation bottomed out in ...
数字(情况)在……达到底部。

(46) The figures reached the bottom / a low point / a trough.
数字(情况)达到底部(低谷)。

(47) a is ... times as much/many as b.
a 是 b 的……倍。

(48) a increased by ...
a 增长了……

(49) a increased to ...
a 增长到……

(50) high/low/great/small/ percentage.
比例高/低

(51) There is an upward trend in the number of ...
……数字呈上升趋势。

(52) a considerable increase/decrease occurred from ... to ...
……到……急剧上升。

(53) From ... to ... the rate of decrease slowed down.
从……到……下降速率减慢。

(54) From that year on, there was a gradual decline/reduction in the ... reaching a figure of ...
从这年起……逐渐下降至……

(55) be similar to ...
与……相似

(56) be the same as ...
与……相同

(57) There are a lot of similarities/differences between ... and ...
……与……之间有许多相似(不同)之处。

(58) a has something in common with b.
a 与 b 有共同之处。

(59) The difference between a and b lies in ...
   a 与 b 之间的差别在于……

(60) ... (year) witnessed/saw a sharp rise in ...
   ……年……急剧上升

7.4 COMMUNICATION LABORATORY

(1) You are Sally Brown, working for Harris & Sons Ltd. Your company is interviewing for a new assistant. Your manager, Miss Anna McDonald, has asked you to help and has given you her notes about the candidates and arrangements. Use the notes below to generate an Interview Programme Form.

Notes for Interviews

We've shortlisted 4 candidates—2 boys and 2 girls. There's Graham Matthews—he works part-time at present for Status Carriers. George Foster is a college graduate who has never had a job. The other two are Sarah Jane and Pauline Tate.

Sarah worked for Temple Press up till 6 months ago but then joined Acme Installations where she is now; you already know Pauline—she works downstairs as receptionist.

They're all about the same age. Graham is 23 and George is 2 years younger. The two girls are a year older than George. Any one of them could do the job.

We'll interview in alphabetical order and allow half an hour for each, starting at 9:30. I think a 15-minute break for coffee half way through would be sensible, don't you?

We promised to give them a tour of the works before the interviews, so we need guides. I'll take George—I want to see what questions he asks, as this is his first job. Will you take Graham, please? I'll ask Bob to take Sarah. I don't think Pauline needs a tour, because she works here already.

(2) Represent the following with a chart.

The refrigerator market in X city is mainly composed of Hisense, Siemens, Haier, LG, and Panasonic. They take up different percentages of sales: Hisense 30%, Siemens 26%, Haier 19%, LG 17%, Panasonic 8%.

(3) Read the table on the number of TV sets sold and present it with a line chart.

Day	Number of TV Sets Sold
Sunday	100
Monday	25
Tuesday	38
Wednesday	56
Thursday	65
Friday	80
Saturday	98

(4) Suppose you are Marketing Manager for a smartphone company. You are to give a presentation in Nanjing on the market share of global premium smartphone brands. The following pie graph shows the global premium smartphone shipment market share of 2019 Q1. Please summarize the information and give possible reasons for the situation.

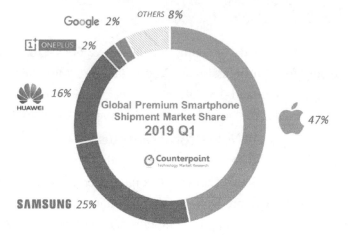

Unit 8　Proposals

8.1　INTRODUCTION

Writing a proposal for a particular purpose such as a project or a curriculum development program is a problem of persuasion. It is good to assume that your reader is a busy, impatient, skeptical person who has no reason to give your proposal special consideration and who is faced with many more requests than he can grant, or even read thoroughly. Such a reader wants to find out quickly and easily the answers to these questions.

- What do you want to do, how much will it cost, and how much time will it take?
- How does the proposed project relate to the company's interests?
- What difference will the project make to your university, your students, your school board, the company, the city, the nation, the world, or whatever the appropriate categories are?
- How do you plan to do it?
- How will the results be evaluated?
- Why should you, rather than someone else, do this project?

These questions will be answered in different ways and receive different emphases depending on the nature of the proposed project and on the agency to which the proposal is being submitted.

8.2　THE PARTS OF A PROPOSAL

The following outline and explanation concern chiefly the components of a project proposal.

8.2.1　Typical Parts of a Project Proposal

- Typical parts of a project proposal are:
- Title (or Cover) Page;
- Summary;
- Introduction (including Statement of Problem, Purpose of Research, and Significance of Research);

- Description of Proposed Research (including Method, Plan or Approach);
- Description of Relevant Institutional Resources;
- Budget;
- Conclusion.

Title (or Cover) Page	Identification of the topic
Summary	Summary of the entire proposal
The Statement of Need	Why this project is necessary
Project Description	Details of how the project will be implemented and evaluated
Budget	Financial description of the project plus explanatory notes
Organization Information	Relevant institutional resources
Conclusion	Summary of the proposal's main points

8.2.2 Presentation of Content

The Title (or Cover) Page. This first page of the proposal is the most important section of the entire document. Here you will provide the reader with a snapshot of what is to follow. Specifically, it summarizes all of the key information and is a sales document designed to convince the reader that this project should be considered for support.

Try to formulate a title with 10 words or less. Use a clear adjective-noun combination to identify the project with its generic class. For example, use "Visual Acuity in Children", rather than "Studies on the Development of Objective Techniques for Monitoring the Development of Visual Acuity in Children". If necessary to further distinguish the focus of the problem, use a subtitle, for example, "Visual Acuity in Infants—Objective Monitoring of its Development".

The Summary. Every proposal, even very brief ones, should have a summary. Some readers read only the summary, and most readers rely on it initially to give them a quick overview of the proposal and later to refresh their memory of its main points.

Each summary should say something about each of the following topics:

- Subject: What is the project about?
- Purposes and significance: Why is the project being done? What is to be accomplished? Why is it important?
- Activities: What will be done? What methods will be used?
- Target population: What special group is being studied or served?
- Location: Where is the work being performed (if different from the location of the principal investigator's organization)?
- Expected outcomes: What types of findings or results will be produced? To whom will these be useful? How will they advance knowledge or the state of the art in your profession?

There are two basic types of abstracts which may be used: descriptive and summary. Most research proposals ask for a summary abstract, while many journals require a descriptive one.

<u>Summary</u>: The summary summarizes the main findings or theories of the proposal or article. The reader can see the projected thrust of the article or project and understands the (potential) outcomes. For example,

> Two principal themes are observed in software development, both aimed at improving the productivity of developing and maintaining new applications. The first is to provide increasingly rich system programming function in order to handle the details of managing hardware resources. The second is to provide application development facilities with logical structures and building blocks more closely aligned with the logic of the application itself. An additional challenge is to provide these in a way that will allow continued enhancement of existing software.

<u>Descriptive</u>: The abstract tells what is in the article or proposal, but it does not offer any conclusions or information about the findings. For example,

> Enormous progress in electronic technology is accelerating the use of computers in everyday life. In this article trends in hardware, input-output technology, computer architecture, software, communications, and artificial intelligence are examined and complexity is identified as a limitation to further progress. Promising directions of research, which may extend the range of computer applications, are discussed.

The Statement of Need. If the reader reads beyond the summary, you have successfully tempered his or her interest. Your next task is to build on this initial interest in your project by enabling the reader to understand the problem that this project will remedy.

The statement of need will enable the reader to learn more about the issues. It presents the facts and evidence that support the need for the project. The information used to support the case can come from authorities in the field, as well as from your company's own experience.

The Description of Proposed Project. The comprehensive explanation of the proposed project is the heart of the proposal and is the primary concern of the readers.

This section of your proposal should have such subsections as objectives, methods, staffing/administration and evaluation. Together, objectives and methods dictate staffing and administrative requirements. They then become the focus of the evaluation to assess the results of the project. Taken together, these subsections present an interlocking picture of the total project.

Objectives. Objectives are the measurable outcomes of the program. They define your methods. Your objectives must be specific, concrete, measurable, and achievable in a specified time period. Some proposal writers often confuse objectives with goals, which are conceptual and more abstract. For the purpose of illustration, here is the goal of a project with a subsidiary objective:

> Goal: Our after-school program will help children read better.
> Objective: Our after-school remedial education program will assist 50 children in improving their reading scores by one grade level as demonstrated on standardized reading tests administered after participating in the program for six months.

The goal in this case is abstract: improving reading, while the objective is much more specific. It is achievable in the short term (six months) and measurable (improving 50 children's reading scores by one grade level).

There are at least four types of objectives:

- Behavioral: A human action is anticipated.

> Example: Fifty of the 70 children participating will learn to swim.

- Performance: A specific time frame within which a behavior will occur, at an expected proficiency level, is expected.

> Example: Fifty of the 70 children will learn to swim within six months and will pass a basic swimming proficiency test administered by a Red Cross-certified lifeguard.

- Process: The manner in which something occurs is an end in itself.

> Example: We will document the teaching methods utilized, identifying those with the greatest success.

- Product: A tangible item results.

> Example: A manual will be created to be used in teaching swimming to this age and proficiency group in the future.

In any given proposal, you will find yourself setting forth one or more of these types of objectives, depending on the nature of your project. Be certain to present the objectives very clearly. Make sure that they do not become lost in verbiage and that they stand out on the page. You might, for example, use numbers, bullets, or indentations to denote the objectives in the text. Above all, be realistic in setting objectives. Don't promise what you can't deliver. Remember, the reader will want to be told in the final report that the project actually accomplished these objectives.

Methods. By means of the objectives, you have explained to the reader what will be achieved by the project. The methods section describes the specific activities that will take place to achieve the objectives. It might be helpful to divide our discussion of methods into the following: how, when, and why.

How: This is the detailed description of what will occur from the time the project begins until it is completed. Your methods should match the previously stated objectives.

When: The methods section should present the order and timing for the tasks. It might make sense to provide a timetable so that the reader does not have to map out the sequencing on his or her own. The timetable tells the reader "when" and provides another summary of the project that supports the rest of the methods section.

Why: You may need to defend your chosen methods, especially if they are new or original. Why will the planned work lead to the outcomes you anticipate? You can answer this question in a number of ways, including using expert testimony and examples of other projects that work.

The methods section enables the reader to visualize the implementation of the project. It should convince the reader that your agency knows what it is doing, thereby establishing its credibility. In describing the methods, you will have mentioned staffing for the project. You now need to devote a few sentences to discussing the number of staff, their qualifications, and specific assignments. Details about individual staff members involved in the project can be included either as part of this section or in the appendix, depending on the length and importance of this information. Describe for the reader your plans for administering the project. This is especially important in a large operation, if more than one agency is collaborating on the project, or if you are using a fiscal agent. It needs to be crystal clear who is responsible for financial management, project outcomes, and reporting.

Evaluation. An evaluation plan should not be considered only after the project is over; it should be built into the project. Including an evaluation plan in your proposal indicates that you take your objectives seriously and want to know how well you have achieved them. Evaluation is also a sound management tool. Like strategic planning, it helps improve its program. An evaluation can often be the best means for others to learn from your experience in conducting the project.

There are two types of formal evaluation. One measures the product; the other analyzes the process. Either or both might be appropriate to your project. The approach you choose will depend on the nature of the project and its objectives. For either type, you will need to describe the manner in which evaluation information will be collected and how the data will be analyzed. You should present your plan for how the evaluation and its results will be reported and the audience to which it will be directed. For example, it might be used internally or be shared with the reader, or it might deserve a wider audience. A reader might even have an opinion about the scope of this dissemination.

The following aspects should be concerned when writing this part:
- Be clear about the focus of the research. In defining the limits of the project, it is helpful to pose the specific question or questions the project is intended to answer.
- Be as detailed as possible about the schedule of the proposed work. When will the first step be completed? When can subsequent steps be started? What must be done before what else, and what can be done at the same time? For complex projects a calendar detailing the projected sequence and interrelationship of events often gives the sponsor assurance that the investigator is capable of careful step-by-step planning.
- Be specific about the means of evaluating the data or the conclusions. Try to imagine the questions or objections of a hostile critic and show that the research plan anticipates them.
- Be certain that the connection between the research objectives and the research method is evident. If a reader fails to see this connection, he will probably not give your proposal any further consideration.

The Budget. Budgets are cost projections. They are also a window into how projects will be implemented and managed. Well-planned budgets reflect carefully thought-out projects. Be sure to only include those things the reader is willing to support.

Readers use these factors to assess budgets:
- Can the job be accomplished with this budget?
- Are costs reasonable for the market or too high or low?
- Is the budget consistent with proposed activities?
- Is there sufficient budget detail and explanation?

Organizational Information. Normally a resume of your organization should come at the end of your proposal. Your natural inclination may be to put this information up front in the document. But it is usually better to sell the need for your project and then your agency's ability to carry it out.

It is not necessary to overwhelm the reader with facts about your organization. This information can be conveyed easily by attaching a brochure or other prepared statement. In two pages or less, tell the reader when your organization came into existence; state its mission, being certain to demonstrate how the subject of the proposal fits within or extends that mission; and describe the organization's structure, programs, and special expertise.

Conclusion. Every proposal should have a concluding paragraph or two. This is a good place to call attention to the future, after the grant is completed. If appropriate, you should outline some of the follow-up activities that might be undertaken to begin to prepare your funders for your next request. Alternatively, you should state how the project might carry on without further support.

This section is also the place to make a final appeal for your project. Briefly reiterate what your nonprofit wants to do and why it is important. Underscore why your agency needs funding to accomplish it. Don't be afraid at this stage to use a bit of emotion to solidify your case.

8.3 SAMPLE PROPOSALS

Sample 8 (1)

January 4, 2007

TO: Ms. Wanda Wise, Director of Corporate Development Black Shoe Company

FROM: Thomas Winston, Project Manager Baxter and Burstein, Management Consultants, Inc.

SUBJECT: Proposal for a Study of Fresno SMSA and Bakersfield SMSA as Possible Location for a New Black Shoe Store

Background

The Black Shoe Company manufactures and markets men's dress shoes in the 70–100 dollar price range. Styles are generally conservative. The shoes are very well made and are entirely repairable, making them unique in today's men's shoe markets.

The Black Shoe Company operates its own retail outlets, an unusual phenomenon in the shoe industry. Most of the stores are located in the East and Midwest, but the company is interested in further expansion in the state of California. Present California stores are located in Los Angeles, San Francisco, San Diego, and Sacramento, the four largest market areas in the state.

The company would like to open a new store in one of the state's smaller market areas. Such a store would not only increase the company's sales, but it would also serve as a test case to help determine the feasibility of further expansion into other smaller California market areas. The cities of Fresno and Bakersfield have been selected by the company as alternative locations for the new store.

Statement of the Problem

The problem is that the company lacks the information necessary to make a comparison between Fresno and Bakersfield as potential market areas. Although the populations of the Fresno and Bakersfield SMSAs are comparable, at 515,013 and 403,089, respectively, little is known about the specific market potentials of the two areas for Black Shoes. (The SMSA, or Standard Metropolitan Statistical Area, is a geographical unit used by the Census Bureau and others in market studies. The Fresno SMSA includes all of Fresno County, and the Bakersfield SMSA includes all of Kern County, where Bakersfield is located.)

Information is needed to compare the relative potential of the markets in Fresno and Bakersfield for conservative men's dress shoes in a relatively high price range. Information is also needed about the present level of competition in the men's shoe business in the two markets. Finally, since this new store will serve as a test of the market for Black Shoes in medium-sized California SMSAs, information is needed to make comparisons between Fresno and Bakersfield and other smaller California market areas.

Goal of the Project

The goal of this study is to provide a recommendation, supported by statistical information, of either Fresno of Bakersfield as the better location for a new Black Shoe Store. Information in support of this recommendation will be drawn from published statistics and other sources available locally. Following an evaluation of the material in this study, the company may wish to arrange for an on-site investigation of the two cities, but such an investigation will not be included in this study.

Research Plan

The information presented in this report will be gathered entirely from publications of the United States Census Bureau, the Department of Commerce, and other sources that may be located during the course of the investigation. Since only preliminary reports of the 1980 Census of the Population are now available, most Census information will be taken from earlier reports.

Such information will support a preliminary recommendation of the better location for the new store and will serve as an excellent background to any subsequent on-site investigation of the two cities that may be commissioned. Since local libraries have excellent collections of governmental publications and other reference materials, no travel will be necessary in this study.

The Cost of the Project

Because of the nature of this problem, the only item of cost is the hourly billing for the researcher's time. The following rough estimates will indicate tentatively the cost of the project:

Preliminary planning and interviews with Black Shoe Company personnel	5 hours
Investigation of Census Bureau sources of information	10 hours
Investigation of other published sources of information	10 hours
Preparation of graphic materials	5 hours
Preparation of final report	10 hours
Presentation of report to Black Shoe Company	5 hours
Total	45 hours

At an average billing rate of $75.00 an hour, the total cost of this project is estimated at $3,375.00.

Sample 8 (2)

A Proposal to Research the Storage Facility for Spenting Nuclear Fuel at Yucca Mountain

Roger Bloom
October 1997

Introduction

Nuclear power plants produce more than 20 percent of the electricity used in the United States (Murray, 1989). Unfortunately, nuclear fission, the process used to create this large amount of energy, creates significant amounts of high level radioactive waste. More than 30,000 metric tons of nuclear waste have arisen from U.S. commercial reactors as well as high level nuclear weapons waste, such as uranium and plutonium (Roush, 1995). Because of the build-up of this waste, some power plants will be forced to shut down. To avoid losing an important source of energy, a safe and economical place to keep this waste is necessary. This document proposes a literature review of whether Yucca Mountain is a suitable site for a nuclear waste repository. The proposed review will discuss the economical and environmental aspects of a national storage facility. This proposal includes my methods for gathering information, a schedule for completing the review, and my qualifications.

Statement of Problem

On January 1, 1998, the Department of Energy (DOE) must accept spent nuclear fuel from commercial plants for permanent storage (Clark, 1997). However, the DOE is undecided on where to put this high level radioactive waste. Yucca Mountain, located in

Nevada, is a proposed site.

There are many questions regarding the safety of the Yucca Mountain waste repository. Researchers at Los Alamos National Laboratory disagree over the long-term safety of the proposed high level nuclear waste site located in Nevada. In 1994, Charles Bowman, a researcher at Los Alamos, developed a theory claiming that years of storing waste in the mountain may actually start a nuclear chain reaction and explode, similar to an atomic bomb (Taubes, 1995). The stir caused by theory suggests that researchers have not explored all sides of the safety issue concerning potentially hazardous situations at Yucca Mountain.

Bowman's theory that Yucca Mountain could explode is based upon the idea that enough waste will eventually disperse through the rock to create a critical mass. A critical mass is an amount of fissile material, such as plutonium, containing enough mass to start a neutron chain reaction (Murray, 1989). Bowman argues that if this chain reaction were started underground, the rocks in the ground would help keep the system compressed and speed up the chain reaction (Taubes, 1995). A chain reaction formed underground could then generate huge amounts of energy in a fraction of a second, resulting in a nuclear blast. A nuclear explosion of this magnitude would emit large amounts of radioactivity into the air and ground water.

Another safety concern is the possibility of a volcanic eruption in Yucca Mountain. The long-term nuclear waste storage facility needs to remain stable for at least 10,000 years to allow the radioactive isotopes to decay to natural levels (Clark, 1997). There are at least a dozen young volcanoes within 40 kilometers of the proposed Yucca Mountain waste site (Weiss, 1996). The proximity of Yucca Mountain to these volcanoes makes it possible to have a volcanic eruption pass through the spent fuel waste repository. Such a volcanic eruption could release damaging amounts of radioactivity to the environment.

Objectives

I propose to review the available literature about using Yucca Mountain as a possible repository for spent nuclear fuel. In this review I will achieve the following two goals:

(1) To explain the criteria for a suitable repository of high-level radioactive waste;

(2) To determine whether Yucca Mountain meets these criteria.

According to the Department of Energy (DOE), a repository for high-level radioactive waste must meet several criteria including safety, location, and economics (Roush, 1995). Safety includes not only the effect of the repository on people near the site, but also people along the transportation routes to the site. In my research I will consider both groups of people. As far as location, a waste site cannot be in an area with a large population or near a ground water supply. Also, because one of the most significant factors in determining the life span of a possible repository is how long the waste storage canisters will remain in tact, the waste site must be located in a dry climate to eliminate the moisture that can cause the waste canisters to corrode. The economics involved in selecting a site is another criterion. At present, the Department of Energy (DOE) has spent more than 1.7 billion dollars on the Yucca Mountain project (Taubes, 1995). For that reason, much pressure exists to select Yucca Mountain as a repository site; otherwise, this money would have been wasted. Other costs, though, have to be considered. For instance, how economical is it to transport radioactive waste across several states to a single national site? I will try to account for as many of these other costs as possible.

After explaining the criteria, I will assess how well Yucca Mountain meets those criteria. In this assessment, I will not assign a numerical score for each criterion. Rather, I will discuss qualitatively how well Yucca Mountain meets each criterion. In some situations, disagreement exists among experts as to how well Yucca Mountain meets a criterion. In such cases, I will present both sides. In this assessment, only Yucca Mountain will be considered as a possible site. Although many sites in the United States could meet the DOE's established criteria, I will consider only Yucca Mountain because the DOE is considering only Yucca Mountain (Taube, 1995).

Plan of Action

This section presents my plan for obtaining the objectives discussed in the previous section. There has been an increase of interest in the nuclear industry concerning the Yucca Mountain site because of the January 1, 1998, deadline for the DOE. Several journal articles and papers discussing the possibility of Yucca Mountain as a spent fuel repository in our near future have surfaced as a consequence of that interest. These articles and books about the dangers of nuclear waste should provide sufficient information for me to complete my review. The following two paragraphs will discuss how I will use these sources in my research.

The first goal of my research is to explain the criteria for determining whether a nuclear waste repository is suitable. For example, will the rock structure be able to withstand human invasion in the future (Clark, 1997)? What will happen if the waste containers corrode and do not last as long as predicted? Will the natural setting contain the waste? To achieve this goal, I will rely on "Background on 40 CFR Part 197 Environmental Standards for Yucca Mountain" (Clark, 1997), the DOE Yucca Mountain home page (1997), and the book *Understanding Radioactive Waste* (Murray, 1989).

A second goal of my literature review is to evaluate Yucca Mountain meets those criteria. I will base my evaluation on the sources mentioned above as well as specific Environmental Protection Agency standards. I also intend to research the validity of possible environmental disasters, such as the explosion theory. To accomplish this goal, I will rely on the paper presented by Clark (1997), and on the book *Blowup at Yucca Mountain* (Taubes, 1995).

Because engineering students are the primary audience for my proposed research topic and may not be familiar with the history of nuclear waste, I will provide a background on past methods used for waste storage. People in the nuclear field with some knowledge of the waste problem facing the industry may be a secondary audience.

Management Plan

This section presents my schedule, costs, and qualifications for completing the proposed research. This research culminates in a formal report, which will be completed by December 5, 1997. To reach this goal, I will follow the schedule presented in Figure 1. Since I already possess literature on the subject of Yucca Mountain as a nuclear waste site, most of my time will be spent sorting through the literature to find key results, and presenting those results to the audience.

The formal presentation will be on October 27, and the formal report will be completed by December 5.

Given that all my sources are available through the University of Wisconsin library system, there is no appreciable cost associated with performing this review, unless one takes into consideration the amount of tuition spent on maintaining the university libraries. The only other minor costs are photocopying articles, creating transparencies for my presentation, printing my report, and binding my report. I estimate these expenses will not exceed $20.

I am a senior in the Engineering Physics Department at the University of Wisconsin at Madison, majoring in nuclear engineering and physics. I have taken several classes related to nuclear waste, economics, and environmental studies. I believe that these courses will aid me in preparing the proposed review. For further information about my qualifications, see the attached resume.

Conclusion

More than 30,000 metric tons of nuclear waste have arisen from U. S. commercial reactors as well as high level nuclear weapons waste, such as uranium and plutonium (Roush, 1995). This document has proposed research to evaluate the possibility of using Yucca Mountain as a possible repository for this spent nuclear fuel. The proposed research will achieve the following goals: (1) explain the criteria necessary to make a suitable high level radioactive waste repository, and (2) determine if Yucca Mountain meets these criteria. The research will include a formal presentation on November 11 and a formal report on December 5.

References

Clark, Raymond L., "Background on 40 CFR Part 197 Environmental Radiation Protection Standards for Yucca Mountain", Proceedings of the 1997 Waste Management Conference (Washington, D. C.: U. S. Environmental Protection Agency, 1997).

Kerr, R., "New Way to Ask the Experts: Rating Radioactive Waste Risks", Science, Vol. 274, (November 1996), pp. 913 – 914.

Murray, Raymond L., Understanding Nuclear Waste (Battelle Press, 1989).

Roush, W., "Can Nuclear Waste Keep Yucca Mountain Dry and Safe?" Science, Vol. 270, (December 1995), pp. 1761 – 1762.

Taubes, G., "Blowup at Yucca Mountain", Science, Vol. 268, (June 1995), pp. 1836 – 1839.

8.4 NOTES

(1) How to begin your proposal
- Thank you for choosing ABC Electronics.
- I am enclosing our proposal for the upgrading of your warehouse security system.
- Thank you for giving NDC Security Systems this opportunity to inspect your plant and recommend a solution.

(2) How to support your proposal and emphasize customer benefits
- I recommend our new XXX Alarm System, which has worked well with other companies like yours.
- There is a 10% discount if you pay for the year's service in advance.
- Our Operating Leases allow qualified corporate customers to obtain off-balance sheet financing.
- This lease structure enables a company to meet its short-term computer needs.
- A short lease term can allow a company to keep pace with technological changes and avoid equipment obsolescence.

(3) How to talk about terms
- We would like the service to be paid within 30 days of completion, rather than the ×× days you suggested.
- I would like to recommend a 3-year operating lease at a monthly rate of 2.5% for the full system.
- For your convenience, we will continue the service unless we hear from you.
- You may discontinue the service at any time.

(4) How to end your proposal and suggest further contact
- I hope this new proposal meets your needs and your budget.
- We look forward to working more closely with you.
- We are looking forward to a smooth start-up.
- I will call you next Monday to discuss how we might proceed.
- I will call you tomorrow to set up a schedule for further discussion.

8.5 COMMUNICATION LABORATORY

Imagine you are dean of International Studies, WXY University and you write a letter to Dr. Allen Burris, Vice President, Meredith College about a Summer Session at XYZ for Meredith College Students.

> Dear Dr. Burris,
>
> At the party held at Dr. Happer's house the evening before I left Raleigh, I mentioned to you my interest in Meredith sending students to XYZ for summer sessions. After I returned, I talked to the department concerned. Each is positive to my suggestion. Investigations have convinced me that XYZ is capable of starting the new program with Meredith College. Here I formally make the proposal to start the program next spring. I believe that you, as one of the founders of the relationship between the two schools, will certainly be happy to see the exchange between the two schools extend into a new area. I hope that you will give careful consideration to my proposal and help facilitate its success with your prestige and influence.
>
> Sincerely yours,

Please write a program proposal with the following information:

Summer Session Time Length

From late May or early June to early or middle of July

Summer Session Arrangement

Dalian (4 weeks): classes of Chinese language and culture on weekdays, sightseeing on weekends

A city in Liaoning Province (1 week): visiting scenic spots

Beijing (1 week): the Great Wall, the Ming Tomb, the Forbidden City and the Summer Palace

Appendix

Charge Table (for each person in US $)

- Four weeks in Dalian

Tuition	300
Registration	50
Housing (10/day × 28)	280
City transportation	100
Textbooks	15
Meals (10/day × 28)	280
Sightseeing tickets	40
Total	995

- One week in Shenyang and Benxi

City to city transportation	110
Housing (40/day × 6)	240
City transportation	90
Meals (15/day × 7)	105
Sightseeing tickets	30
Total	575

- One week in Beijing

Housing	240
City transportation	60
Meals (15/day × 6)	90
Sightseeing tickets	40
Total	430
Altogether	2,000

Note: The suggested charges are negotiable with the fluctuations of the exchange rate.

Unit 9　Reports

A report, a detailed account of a particular matter, is used to relay information from one person to another. Reports play an important role in business practice as corporations usually make decisions on the basis of those reports.

9.1　CATEGORIES OF REPORTS

Business reports can be either written or oral. The reports in written form, which is more often used, serve not only as a way of relaying information but also as official records of the information relayed.

Business reports can be classified according to their different contents. There are routine reports, investigative reports, progress reports, and feasibility reports. A routine report is a report presented to upper management on the day-to-day work; an investigative report is the description of the findings of an investigation; a progress report provides information of an ongoing program; a feasibility report is an assessment of the practicality of a proposed plan or method. Other kinds of reports include incident reports, supervision reports, sales reports, improvement reports, market studies and research reports.

Business reports that are one—three pages long fall into the category of short reports, while those longer belong to the category of long reports. The short report form is more widely used in writing incident reports, progress reports, supervision reports, sales reports, and improvement reports. Long reports are often found in research reports, market studies, and feasibility reports.

Business reports can also be typed in their styles. Some reports are in the form of letters, others in the form of memos, still others in the form of documents. Generally speaking, short business reports are often in the form of memos or letters, while most long business reports are in the form of documents.

Some business reports are called informational reports because the main function of them is to relay or provide information. Other business reports are called analytical reports because they are written to report the findings of certain investigations, to describe the analysis of those findings, and to present recommendations on how to solve those problems.

9.2 STEPS OF REPORT WRITING

There are generally three steps in the course of writing a business report.

The first step is to get fully prepared for the report writing. The writer should first identify what purpose the report is for, to whom the report is sent, what kind of relationship is between him and the sent-to-person, and how much background information the sent-to-person has about the report. Taking all these factors into account, the writer can decide on the right length and tone of the report.

Next is the step of collecting data. Writing of a report should be based on sufficient information and facts relevant to it. The data can be collected through the author's own observations, surveys, interviews, quotations of some other authoritative reports, or publications.

Before starting to write a report, an outline of it should be drafted to further clarify the main points of the report. In the course of writing a report, the writer should make sure:

- The subject of the report is focused on.
- The purpose of the report is worthwhile.
- The appropriate format is used for the report.
- All problems involved are identified in the report.
- The facts are presented objectively.
- Conclusions are drawn and recommendations are put forward on the basis of the data collected and the analysis made.

To add to the credibility of a report, the data used in it should be correct and authoritative. Besides to illustrate the points clear, figures and tables are often used in reports.

9.3 THE LAYOUT OF REPORTS

Short business reports and long business reports are different in their structures.

9.3.1 Short Reports

Short reports are more commonly used in business, for they are everyday working reports. Short reports can be written in different formats. However, most short reports consist of four sections: introduction, findings, conclusion and recommendations.

The first section of a short report is the introduction. In this part background information of the report is described, the purpose of the report is identified, the main contents are illustrated and the research methods are explained.

Following the first section is that of findings, where findings of the research or investigation are described. This is the core part of a report. In this section the subject of the report is discussed in detail, the data collected during the research or investigation are listed and analyzed, and solutions to the problems involved are presented.

In the section of conclusion the major results of the research or investigation are summed up and a conclusion is drawn.

The last section is that of recommendations. Based on the findings of the research and analysis of those findings, suggestion is put forward for the reference of the individual receiving the report.

9.3.2 Long Reports

A long report takes a more formal form. Usually it is composed of seven parts: the Title Fly, the Title Page, the Letter of Transmittal, the Executive Summary, the Table of Contents, the Body, the Appendix and the Bibliography.

The Title Fly or the Cover Page is optional, but it can add to the formality of the report. Like the cover of a book, it contains the title of the report and the author's name.

The Title Page begins with the title of the report. Below it come the phrase "Prepared for" or "Submitted to" and the name, title and organization of the sent-to-person. Further below are the phrase "Prepared by" or "Submitted by" and the author's name and title, followed by the date when the report is submitted.

The Letter of Transmittal is a letter to the person to whom the report is submitted. It usually carries brief information of the report's subject, how it was authorized, how it has been worked out and also some personal viewpoints on certain subjects. The Letter of Transmittal usually ends with appreciation for the assignment, instruction for the reader's follow-up actions, acknowledgements of the help from others and offers of assistance in answering questions.

The Executive Summary is an abstract of the report. A well-done summary can make clear the main ideas of the report to the person who reads it. It is aimed to present, in very accurate and brief language, the facts on which the report is based, the ways of collecting data, the conclusion drawn and the author's viewpoints, as well as some recommendations. The appropriate length of an executive summary is about 5% or 10% of that of the report.

The Table of Contents gives out the main sections and subsections of the report, including a tabular arrangement to indicate the headings used in the report. For short reports all headings are included while for long reports only first and second-level headings are listed. Besides for reports with several figures, a List of Figure is needed to help readers locate them, for each figure is indicated its title and page number.

The Body, the core part of a report, usually consists of three sections: an introduction identifying the report's purpose and scope; a central part discussing the report's findings objectively; a final part stating the conclusions or putting forward some recommendations.

The body of a long report begins with an introduction. The introduction may include the background knowledge of the report, the problem or purpose which motivates the report, the significance, the scope, and the structure of the report. In other words, this

part centers on answering the following three questions:
- Why is the report written?
- What is contained in the report?
- How is the report written?

The central part is the principle section of a report. In this section the writer discusses, analyzes, interprets, and evaluates the research findings and presents solutions to the problems involved.

The conclusion part interprets the findings, in terms of how they are related to the solutions to the original problem.

Some reports include a recommendation section. In this section, recommendations are submitted on actions to solve the problem.

The Appendix contains documents related to the report but not included in the body part of the report. Those often included in an appendix are questionnaires, statistical formulas, and glossaries of terms. If there are several appendices in a report, they should be arranged in the same order as that in the body text.

The Bibliography lists all the references and sources of information along with background or recommended reading in an alphabetical order. Each item includes the author, title, date of publication, page number for magazine article, and some other significant information.

Hereunder are some useful expressions for report writing.

* The purpose/aim of this report is to ...
* The report aims to ...
* The main purpose of the report is to present a methodology to carry the study on ...
* The objective of this study is to ...
* This report sets out the reasons why ...
* This report presents ...
* The report you asked me to prepare on ... has revealed some interesting findings.
* The report is based on the information we collected ...
* The report carries information on ...
* To ... the following questions must be answered.
* This report is concerned with ...
* This report will continue as follows. First, ... Second, ...
* As you requested, we have done a comprehensive analysis of ...
* Here are the results of ... you requested.
* Both primary and secondary data are used in this research to analyze ...
* The following section explains the methodology that was used in this report.
* A questionnaire survey was conducted to learn about ...
* Current business periodicals and newspapers were consulted for background information.
* The key findings are outlined below.
* It was found that ...

* The following findings summarize our key findings.
* It is clear that ...
* No conclusions were reached regarding ...
* It was agreed that ...
* It was found that ...
* It was felt that ...
* We discovered that ...
* Most people thought that ...
* Based on the findings of ..., the following conclusions can be drawn.
* It would be advisable to ...
* It is essential to ...
* We strongly recommend that ...
* We put forward the following recommendations.
* We recommend ...
* The literature review supports the following recommendations.
* Supported by the findings and conclusions of this study, the following recommendations are offered.
* There are a number of reasons for ...
* There are several factors which affect ...

9.4 SAMPLE REPORTS

Sample 9 (1)

A short annual report

Simens

The results of the 1st quarter of fiscal year 2006 demonstrate that Fit4More is working. For example, the action plan sets an ambitious goal of growing at twice the rate of the GDP in our markets. We exceeded that goal with order increases of 31% over last year's first quarter, thanks to some impressive new business wins. We won a EUR 669 million order for high speed trains in China as well as an order for transformer stations for Qatar worth almost EUR 500 million. In Germany, we secured an order to supply radio link technology worth some EUR 250 million.

We've also continued the important strategic reorientation of our portfolio by taking further steps to strengthen Com and SBS. We sold the Product Related Services (PRS) business of SBS, a EUR 1.3 billion business that primarily offers lower end IT services to Fujitsu Siemens Computers. The 5,000 PRS employees now have an opportunity to work in a company where this type of service is critically important. And SBS will be able to focus on IT outsourcing and innovative IT solutions, businesses where Siemens can offer a competitive advantage.

Orders growth and strategic reorientation are components of the "Performance and

Portfolio" platform of Fit4More. In the first quarter we also had progress in the other three Fit4More platforms. In October, we recognized the global winners of the top + best practices awards, highlighting programs that will serve as models for the "Operational Excellence" platform. Our innovative power showed in the first quarter as well: For example, we presented our new Computer Tomography device which leads to pictures quicker and with less impact on the patient. We also launched the first Leadership Excellence sessions, a key part of our "People Excellence" platform indispensable to transforming Siemens into a high performance organization. Within the "Corporate Responsibility" platform, we strengthened our sustainability positioning by buying a leading pollution control supplier to the coal industry and expanding our wind power and water businesses.

Since "actions speak louder than words", those successes make discussions at the annual meeting easier. But there is still much more to be done, particularly in improving our cash management and in achieving target profit margins in several groups. In my next regular letter, in April when I share with you the results of the 2nd quarter, I hope to report progress in profitability and cash management. Until then, I hope you will help me meet our commitments to execute decisively our Fit4More strategy.

Sample 9 (2)

A feasibility report

Laptop Computer Purchase

This is a feasibility report on the purchase of a laptop computer for the Software of the Future Company. The Software of the Future Company owns numerous IBM PS/2 computers which are adequate for the needs of the company for use in the office. However, there are many occasions where a smaller, portable laptop computer would be very useful. There are many occasions where employees would like to take a computer with them to a customer's office, either to a prospective customer's office for demonstrations of past work or to a current customer's office for demonstrations of work in process. There are also many occasions when it would be useful for employees to be able to take home a laptop computer with them for use in finishing work that is on a time schedule or for use when circumstances demand that they cannot come into work, but would be able to do some work while at home. The purchase of a laptop computer would need to take into consideration the following criteria:
- IBM-PC AT-compatibility
- Size of the machine, weight, portability, and battery power
- RAM memory size of the machine, disk space, disk drives
- Quality and readability of the display screen
- Cost of the machine

The laptop would need to be compatible with the IBM PS/2 computers in the office.

This would mean that it would need to have a 3-1/2 inch microfloppy disk drive. The laptop would need to be small in size, light enough to be carried comfortably for extended amounts of time and have enough battery power to last through a 1-to-2-hour presentation without the screen dimming or the processing slowing down. The laptop would need to have enough RAM memory to run large programs, a minimum of 1000K. A hard disk drive of 20 megabytes would be very useful, but not entirely necessary. If a hard disk drive is included in the machine, one disk drive would be adequate; otherwise, two disk drives would be required. The screen of the laptop would need to be of average to good quality so that it would not be a strain for customers or employees to view the screen. Cost is not the most important criteria for the selection of the laptop, but a price range of $1,000 to $2,000 should be considered.

Comparisons

There are many reliable laptop computers currently on the market. Some of the best on the market are the Zenith SuperSportSX and the Toshiba T3100SX, which are the first battery-powered 80386SX based portable computers on the market. These machines have a 16 MHz clock speed and both include a 40 megabyte hard drive. However, the price of these two machines each run into approximately $6,000. These machines are the top of the market and are aimed at professionals who need to compute on the go: salespeople, executives, field personnel and journalists, for example (3:96). These are much more than what our needs require. Some of the laptops in our price range include the Toshiba T1200HB, the NEC Multispeed EL-2, the Epson Equity LT, the Tandy 1400LT, the Datavue Spark, the Zenith SuperSport 184-1, and the Toshiba T1000. The NEC Multispeed EL-2, the Epson Equity LT, the Tandy 1400LT, and the Datavue Spark are not going to be considered because they all have less than the 1000K RAM memory requirement and the RAM memory is not expandable at the present time. The three laptops that will be considered further will be the Toshiba T1200HB, the Zenith SuperSport 184-1, and the Toshiba T1000. All three of these machines are compatible with our currently owned IBM PS/2 office computers.

Weight

The Toshiba T1200HB has a weight of 11.1 lbs. The Zenith SuperSport 184-1 has a weight of 14 lbs. The Toshiba T1000 has a weight of 6.2 lbs [1:7:72]. All three machines are light enough and small enough in size to be easily portable. The lighest is the Toshiba T1000, but the heaviest, the Zenith SuperSport 184-1 is still light enough at 14 lbs, to carry without much trouble.

Battery Life

The battery life of the Toshiba T1200HB is 3 hours. The battery life of the Zenith SuperSport 184-1 is 5-1/2 hours and the battery life of the Toshiba T1000 is 5-1/4 hours. The Zenith SuperSport 184-1 has the longest batterylife, but all three laptops have adequate battery life time for our needs.

RAM Memory and Disk Storage

The RAM memory size of the Toshiba T1200HB is 1 megabyte, expandable to 2 megabytes and has a 20 megabyte hard drive. The Zenith SupersPort 184-1 has a RAM memory of 640k, but it is expandable to 1640k and also has a 20 megabyte hard drive. The Toshiba T1000 has a RAM memory size of 512k, expandable to 1280k. The Toshiba T1000 does not have a hard drive available. Both the Toshiba T1200HB and the Zenith SupersPort 184-1 have dual disk drives. The Toshiba T1000 comes with a single disk drive [1:71-72]. The Toshiba T1200HB and the Zenith SupersPort 184-1 are very competitive in RAM memory and disk storage.

Screen Characteristics

The Toshiba T1200HB has good screen quality as far as laptops go. The Zenith SupersPort 184-1 screen is the largest screen among these three laptops, but not very bright or readable in bright light. The Toshiba T1000 screen is a reflective LCD screen which lacks brightness and is small in size, only 3 inches high with 25 lines of text crammed into those 3 inches which makes the characters looked squashed [1:72]. The Toshiba T1200HB has the best quality screen.

Price

The list price of the Toshiba T1200HB is $2,199, but has been advertised for $1,788. The Zenith SupersPort 184-1 has a list price of $3,199 and has been advertised at a price of $2,100. The Toshiba T1000 has a list price of $999 with an advertised price of $598 [1:71-72]. The Zenith SupersPort 184-1 is a little over our price range. The Toshiba T1000 definitely has the lowest price, but it is also a less powerful machine.

Summary

The following is a summary of the comparison of the Toshiba T1200HB, the Zenith SupersPort 184-1, and the Toshiba T1000:

1. All three machines are compatible with the currently owned IBM PS/Ss.
2. The Toshiba T1000 is the lightest of the three computers with a weight of 6.2 lbs.
3. The Zenith SupersPort 184-1 has the longest battery life.
4. The Toshiba T1200HB has the best RAM memory options with 1 megabyte, expandable to 2 megabytes and 20 megabyte hard drive.
5. The Toshiba T1200HB and the Zenith SupersPort 184-1 are equal in disk storage with a 20 megabyte hard drive each.
6. The Toshiba T1200HB has the best screen quality of the three laptops.
7. The Toshiba T1000 definitely has the lowest price of the three laptops, but is not as powerful a machine as the Toshiba T1200HB, which is definitely within the price range and compares favorably in all but the battery life, 3 hours, which is still adequate for our needs.

TABLE 1. Rankings of the Toshiba T1200HB, the Zenith SuperSport 184-1, and the Toshiba T1000. (Rankings: 3 - highest, 2 - middle, 1 - lowest)

Categories of Comparison	Toshiba T1200HB		Zenith Super-Sport 184-1		Toshiba T1000	
Compatibility	yes	3	yes	3	yes	3
Weight (lbs)	11.1	2	14	1	6.2	3
Battery (hrs)	3	1	5.5	3	5.25	2
RAM Memory (KB)	2000	3	1640	2	1280	1
Hard Drive (MB)	20	3	20	3	none	1
Screen Quality	good	3	ave.	2	poor	1
Price	$1,788	2	$2,100	1	$598	3
Total Rankings		17		15		14

Recommendations

Based on the criteria previously discussed in this report and the ratings from Table 1, I recommend the following:

- Purchase a Toshiba T1200HB laptop computer which is within the price range and has the highest among the three laptops compared.
- Do not purchase a laptop at the present time and since the laptop computer industry is a relatively new and changing industry, wait six months and re-evaluated the market at that time.

Sample 9 (3)

A long report

A CONSULTANT DIRECTED PROGRAM

ON INSTRUCTION IN "DELEGATION OF AUTHORITY"

Robert Smith

(The Title Fly)

A CONSULTANT DIRECTED PROGRAM

ON INSTRUCTION IN "DELEGATION OF AUTHORITY"

Prepared for

Mr. William H. Jackson, President

Western Insurance Company

Prepared by

Robert Smith, Assistant

Research Department

Los Angeles, California

Date: June 6, 2021

(The Title Page)

June 6, 2021

Mr. William H. Jackson
President
Western Insurance Company
500 Ewins Road
New York

Dear Mr. Jackson,

    Here is the report you requested on the subject of executive training in delegation of authority. The report presents justifications for the necessity of the program "a seminar conducted by an outside consultant".

    Please do not hesitate to contact me if you have any questions about this report. Thank you very much for assigning me the study.

Yours truly,
Robert Smith
Assistant
Research Department

(The Letter of Transmittal)

Contents

1. Introduction ··· 1
2. A Formal Program of Instruction Is Recommended ·························· 2
3. Cost of Instruction Is Least through Outside Consultants ··················· 3
4. Summary of Reasons for Recommending a Seminar Conducted by Outside Consultants ·· 6
5. Bibliography ··· 7

(Table of Contents)

Introduction

Because of several observations, Western Insurance Company is concerned about the need for increased delegation of authority by its executive staff.

Purpose

This study was designed to answer two questions: 1) Should Western Insurance Company have a formal program of instruction in delegation of authority? 2) if so, what is the preferred method of conducting such a program?

Background

Company officials have posed these questions because of the following observations: 1) Many executives appear overworked and rushed; 2) An executive's absence for illness or vacation disrupts work; 3) many younger workers have left the firm complaining of lack of work, authority, and responsibility; 4) Average claim-adjustment time is 40 days after submission.

For the information of those who do not work directly with branch offices, Western Insurance Company maintains 14 branch offices in 7 states. Branch managers refer all claims to executives in the home office for adjustment.

A Formal Program of Instruction Is Recommended

Western executives have had very little formal instruction in delegation. None has had a college course in delegation. They appear to be somewhat familiar with principles; they admit weakness in application.

If an understanding of the principles were all the Western Insurance executives needed, the firm could supply them with books and magazine articles written on delegation. However, seminars can best contribute to understanding the function of implementation.

Our daily work schedule, then, would be least affected by having executives take management courses at State University night school; but for this advantage, Western Insurance Company would have to pay a higher price.

Cost of Instruction Is Least through Outside Consultants

Of the three approaches to delegation training, outside consultants are the least expensive when only direct instructional costs are considered. Indirect costs are difficult to establish.

Direct Instructional Costs Are Low

The optimum number of participants in any seminar appears to be 10, according to the executives and consultants interviewed. More than 10 executives away from their offices at one time could handicap our daily operations; seminars with more than 10 participants could restrict opportunities for exchanging views. If 50 are to receive instruction, they should be divided into 5 separate groups.

Each of the consultants thought ten 2-hour sessions would be adequate for each group. Each charges a fee of $70 an hour ($1,400 for 20 hours of instruction). Of the half dozen Western executives whose backgrounds and interests are such that they could conduct the seminars, each is earning over $50,000 a year—about $25 an hour. Since none of these men has conducted a previous seminar in delegation, company officials have arrived at a conclusion that for each class hour spent in seminar a company executive would have to spend at least two hours of company time in preparation. Some would probably devote other hours at home. Thus, the cost of 20 hours of seminar would be $1,500. Expenses for supplies and films would be about the same for company instructors as for consultants.

Indirect Instructional Costs Are Low

Technically, costs for on-the-premises instruction should include allowance for use of a conference room, time lost by executives, and interruption of work. However, these factors are discounted because of the difficulty in measuring them.

Cost of Room

Cost of the seminar room was discounted for two reasons: 1) Western maintains a conference room already, and its present schedule is light enough to accommodate delegation seminars without serious scheduling problems; 2) Light or power expenses would be about the same regardless of who is teaching the course.

Lost Time

Cost of lost time was discounted because: 1) as salaried worker, executives may find means of making up for lost time, hopefully, by delegating; and 2) through spending two hours in a single seminar, executives may learn ways to increase their efficiency, thus enabling Western to recoup many times the value of the time lost.

Interruption of Work

Understandably, executives' absences could cause subordinates to lose time in waiting for their return; their absences could cause delays that result in a loss of goodwill. But measuring these factors was too difficult; furthermore, the seminars would be designed to give instruction in surrounding such problems.

Both direct and indirect costs should be regained in terms of dollars saved. The amount of saving realized from instruction in delegation cannot be estimated accurately, but some figures presented in another insurance company's annual report may be helpful. After a formal program of consultant-directed instruction in delegation, the company reported savings far beyond the cost of the program, more time for executives to think and plan, and generally improved morale. No one can tell whether Western would have a similar experience, but similarities in goals and size give much cause for optimism.

Summary of Reasons for Recommending a Seminar

Conducted by Outside Consultants

The following percentages, which authorities say are exceeding high, suggest a need for training in delegation.

1. Almost 90 percent of Western executives spend more time executing details than planning.
2. About 75 percent are frequently interrupted to give advice or make decisions for subordinates.
3. About 75 percent say they have no subordinates whom they trust to make decisions for them.
4. Over 50 percent take work home with them.

A professional consultant is recommended as the preferred means of conducting a training program in delegation because:

1. Consultants can present theoretical principles while pointing out specific applications.
2. Consultants are specialists in seminar instruction.
3. Consultants' advice may be more readily accepted than the advice of fellow executives.

4. Consultant-directed programs are less expensive than either night courses or firm-directed programs.

Bibliography

Lewis, Philip V. Organizational Communication: The Essence of Effective Management, 2nd ed. Columbus, Ohio: Grid publishing, Inc., 1980. John S. Ewing, "Patterns of Delegation". Harvard Business Review, XXXIX, No. 4 (July – August 1961), 33.

Westfield Insurance Company. "Annual Report for 1979", March 1980, 4.

Frederick, Williams. The Communications Revolution. Beverly Hills, California: Sage Publications, 1982.

(Bibliography)

9.5 NOTES

(1) routine report　日常事务报告；例行工作报告
(2) investigation report　调查报告
(3) progress report　进度报告
(4) feasibility report　可行性报告
(5) informational report　信息报告
(6) analytical report　分析报告
(7) incident report　事故报告
(8) supervision report　监督报告
(9) sales report　销售报告
(10) improvement report　改进报告
(11) research report　研究报告
(12) market study　市场研究
(13) title fly　扉页
(14) title page　题名页
(15) letter of transmittal　转送函
(16) executive summary　执行摘要；项目简介
(17) table of contents　目录
(18) body　正文
(19) appendix　附录
(20) bibliography　文献目录

9.6 COMMUNICATION LABORATORY

A. Give a brief answer to the following questions.

(1) What are the differences between long reports and short reports?

(2) What are the major parts of a long report?

(3) What are the role and content of a letter of transmittal?

(4) What is included in the executive summary?

B. Case Study

Write a report to the Students' Affairs Office of your university on the students' assessment of the University's ethical climate.

■ Your report should be based on the questionnaire below and the results you have obtained.

■ To score the questionnaire, first add up your responses to questions 1, 3, 6, 9, 10, and 11. This is subtotal number 1. Next, reverse the scores on questions 2, 4, 5, 7, and 8 (5 = 0, 4 = 1, 3 = 2, 2 = 3, 1 = 4, 0 = 5). Add the reverse scores to form subtotal number 2. Add subtotal number 1 to subtotal number 2 for an overall score.

Subtotal 1 + Subtotal 2 = Overall Score

Overall scores can range from 0 to 55. The higher the score, the more the organization's culture encourages ethical behavior.

Completely false	Mostly false	Somewhat false	Somewhat true	Mostly true	Completely true
0	1	2	3	4	5

1. In this university, people are expected to follow their own personal and moral beliefs.
2. People are expected to do anything to further the university's interests.
3. In this university, people look out for each other's good.
4. It is very important to follow the university's rules and procedures strictly.
5. In this university, people protect their own interests above other considerations.
6. The consideration is whether a decision violates any law.
7. Everyone is expected to stick by university rules and procedures.
8. The most efficient way is always the right way in this university.
9. Our major consideration is what is best for everyone in the university.
10. In this university, the law or ethical code of the profession is the major consideration.
11. It is expected at this university that faculty will always do what is right for the students and the public.

Unit 10 Articles

Articles are usually written for a company magazine, a newsletter, a commemorative programme, or as a submission to a newspaper. They should be narrative, informative and interesting to read. Here are certain article writing strategies you can follow to help you easily create your article.

10.1 THE FORMAT OF BUSINESS ARTICLES

An article normally consists of the following sections:
- Title: that sums up the message of the article;
- Introduction: the first section of an article that includes the topic sentence or opening paragraph that gives background information or provides a transition;
- Body: that follows the introduction, discusses the controlling idea, using facts, arguments, analysis, examples, and other information;
- Conclusion: the final section that summarizes the connections between the information discussed in the body and the controlling idea.

10.2 FOUR-STEP APPROACH FOR ARTICLE WRITING

A four-step approach is recommended when writing a business article:
- Collecting Information
- Planning the Structure
- Writing the Draft
- Proofreading and Editing

Step 1

Before you write the article, it is important to consider who you are writing the article for, and why. Then you may ask yourself the following questions:
- Who wants the article?
- Why do they want it?
- What are they going to do with it?
- What do they want it to cover?
- What will the article not cover?

- What will happen as a result of the article?
- When you collect information, you may check existing knowledge, record the sources used, make notes from the sources, reference sources as you go along, order your notes and group together points based on your original plan.

Step 2

Develop an article outline (i.e., the overall structure of your article) by identifying particular headings and subheadings.

List the ideas associated with each heading and subheading. Group related ideas where possible and then arrange them in a logical order.

Plan the introduction and the conclusion (but do not use phrases such as "The Introduction", "The Conclusion" or "The Main Body" as the headings).

Step 3 and 4

Use the outline you developed in Step 2. Write the first draft.

Develop one paragraph for each idea or topic. Write a strong opening sentence for each paragraph, which will indicate the conclusions you made at the case analysis stage.

Avoid redundant or overblown words.

Be concise! When 6 words will replace 14 words, let them do so!

Check grammar, spelling, and punctuation.

Number the pages.

Write Draft 2 and correct for errors, wordiness and unnecessarily pretentious words.

Proofread Draft 2. It's a good idea to have another person do this.

10.3 WRITING GUIDE

10.3.1 Title

Choosing the title of your article will be one of the most important decisions you will make. You need to take your time, when it comes for you to select an article title and it will require you to do some brainstorming.

An article should have a short, straightforward title directed at the general reader. Lengthy systematic names and complicated and numerous chemical formulae should therefore be avoided where possible. The use of non-standard abbreviations and symbols in a title is not encouraged. Brevity in a title, though desirable, should be balanced against its accuracy and usefulness.

China Becomes the Second Largest Auto Parts Exporter to the U.S.

This is the title of an article published by Agence France-Presse. It mirrors the message of the article and is thus a good title.

10.3.2 Introduction

An appropriate introduction to the article encourages a reader to continue reading.

You have competition for the reader's time, so let them know right away what they will get if they read your piece. Try to stay at most with three sentences in your opening paragraph. For example,

---

China Becomes the Second Largest Auto Parts Exporter to the U. S.

June 8, 2007—China replaced Germany in the first quarter as the second largest auto parts exporter to the U. S., Chinese state media said. In the first three months of the year, China exported $1.936 billion worth of auto parts to the United States, up 27.4% one year, the Shanghai Securities News reported, citing figures from the U. S. Department of Commerce.

10.3.3 A Body of Paragraphs and Topic Sentences

A paragraph is a series of sentences that are organized and coherent, and are all related to a single topic. Almost every piece of writing you do that is longer than a few sentences should be organized into paragraphs. This is because paragraphs show a reader where the subdivisions of an essay begin and end, and thus help the reader see the organization of the essay and grasp its main points.

Paragraphs can contain many different kinds of information. A paragraph could contain a series of brief examples or a single long illustration of a general point. It might describe a place, character, or process; narrate a series of events; compare or contrast two or more things; classify items into categories; or describe causes and effects. Regardless of the kind of information they contain, all paragraphs share certain characteristics. One of the most important of these is a topic sentence.

A well-organized paragraph supports or develops a single controlling idea, which is expressed in a sentence called the topic sentence. A topic sentence has several important functions: it substantiates or supports an essay's thesis statement; it unifies the content of a paragraph and directs the order of the sentences; and it advises the reader of the subject to be discussed and how the paragraph will discuss it. Readers generally look at the first few sentences in a paragraph to determine the subject and perspective of the paragraph. That's why it's often best to put the topic sentence at the very beginning of the paragraph. In some cases, however, it's more effective to place another sentence before the topic sentence—for example, a sentence linking the current paragraph to the previous one, or one providing background information.

The following paragraph illustrates this pattern of organization. In this paragraph the topic sentence and concluding sentence (capitalized) both help the reader keep the paragraph's main point in mind.

SCIENTISTS HAVE LEARNED TO SUPPLEMENT THE SENSE OF SIGHT IN NUMEROUS WAYS. In front of the tiny pupil of the eye they put, on Mount Palomar, a great monocle 200 inches in diameter, and with it see 2,000 times farther into the depths of space. Or they look through a small pair of lenses arranged as a microscope into a drop of water or blood, and magnify by as much as 2,000 diameters the living creatures there, many of which are among man's most dangerous enemies. Or, if we want to see distant happenings on earth, they use some of the previously wasted electromagnetic waves to carry television images which they re-create as light by whipping tiny crystals on a screen with electrons in a vacuum. Or they can bring happenings of long ago and far away as colored motion pictures, by arranging silver atoms and color-absorbing molecules to force light waves into the patterns of original reality. Or if we want to see into the center of a steel casting or the chest of an injured child, they send the information on a beam of penetrating short-wave X-rays, and then convert it back into images we can see on a screen or photograph. THUS ALMOST EVERY TYPE OF ELECTROMAGNETIC RADIATION YET DISCOVERED HAS BEEN USED TO EXTEND OUR SENSE OF SIGHT IN SOME WAY.

Although most paragraphs should have a topic sentence, there are a few situations when a paragraph might not need a topic sentence. For example, you might be able to omit a topic sentence in a paragraph that narrates a series of events, if a paragraph continues developing an idea that you introduced (with a topic sentence) in the previous paragraph, or if all the sentences and details in a paragraph clearly refer—perhaps indirectly—to a main point. The vast majority of your paragraphs, however, should have a topic sentence.

10.3.4 Conclusion

This should be easy because you are re-capping what you just wrote about. If you are promoting a product or service, we find that leaving a question, or giving the reader a teaser of something more is very helpful. We know it isn't proper "etiquette", but it helps in leaving the reader wanting more.

China Becomes the Second Largest Auto Parts Exporter to the U. S.

June 8, 2007—China replaced Germany in the first quarter as the second largest auto parts exporter to the US, Chinese state media said. In the first three months of the year, China exported $1.936 billion worth of auto parts to the United States, up 27.4% one year, the Shanghai Securities News reported, citing figures from the US Department of Commerce.

That is two million dollars more than exports from Germany, but still a distant second Japan with $3.57 billion, the report said.

In the first four months this year, China exported a total of $3.6 billion worth of auto parts globally, a surge of 34.8% year on year, and imports stood at $3.5 billion, up 25.9%.

However, analysts argued higher exports did not necessarily translate into stronger competitiveness as profit margins of German-made auto parts were much larger than Chinese products.

The robust growth of China's auto parts exports has been bolstered mainly by cheaper labor costs, lower raw material prices and looser environmental restrictions, according to a previous report by *The New York Times*. But these advantages may not be sustainable as wages are rising and the government tightens controls on pollution and exports of resources, the newspaper said.

10.3.5 Techniques for Coherent Paragraphs

A number of techniques that you can use to establish coherence in paragraphs are described below.

Repeat key words or phrases. Particularly in paragraphs in which you define or identify an important idea or theory, be consistent in how you refer to it. This consistency and repetition will bind the paragraphs together and help your reader understand your definition or description.

Create parallel structures. Parallel structures are created by constructing two or more phrases or sentences that have the same grammatical structure and use the same parts of speech. By creating parallel structures you make your sentences clearer and easier to read. In addition, repeating a pattern in a series of consecutive sentences helps your reader see the connections between ideas. In the paragraph above about scientists and the sense of sight, several sentences in the body of the paragraph have been constructed in a parallel way. The parallel structures (which have been emphasized) help the reader see that the paragraph is organized as a set of examples of a general statement.

Be consistent in point of view, verb tense, and number. Consistency in point of view, verb tense, and number is a subtle but important aspect of coherence. If you shift from the more personal "you" to the impersonal "one", from past to present tense, or from "a man" to "they", for example, you make your paragraph less coherent. Such inconsistencies can also confuse your reader and make your argument more difficult to follow.

Use transitional words or phrases between sentences and between paragraphs. Transitional expressions emphasize the relationships between ideas, so they help readers follow your train of thought or see connections that they might otherwise miss or misunderstand.

10.4 SAMPLE ARTICLES

Sample 10 (1)

Will China Face an Oversupply of Petrochemicals in the Coming Years?

Shanghai. May 30. INTERFAX-CHINA—Petrochemical production capacity in Asia, and the Middle East in particular, is currently expanding at a rapid rate in order to meet soaring demand from China, leading to speculation that the country could face a flood of cheap petrochemical imports in coming years.

At an energy forum held in Shanghai recently, industry insiders were unable to agree on whether or not China will face such a situation. Some argued that if Middle Eastern countries continue to expand their production capacity, or if the Chinese economy fails to sustain its present runaway growth, China will face oversupply in the market as early as 2010.

On the other hand, others maintained that demand for basic petrochemical products such as ethylene will continue to outpace any increase in supply, but that the region's traditional petrochemical exporters, such as Japan and Korea, will face increasingly fierce competition from their aggressive counterparts in the Middle East.

With plans underway to add 23 million tons a year in ethylene cracker capacity between 2006 and 2010, Middle Eastern countries such as Saudi Arabia, Iran and Qatar, will be able to produce 30 million tons of ethylene annually by 2010, according to Liu Jie, deputy chief economist of the PetroChina Chemicals & Marketing Co. Approximately 80 percent of the ethylene to be produced is intended for export, Liu added.

Over the same period, Asia-Pacific countries other than China will increase their refining capacity by 1.6 million barrels a day to reach a daily output of 18.4 million barrels. The highest growth in capacity will be seen in India, with the country to account for 62 percent of the region's capacity expansion.

China's frenzied expansion of its own production capacity has also added to oversupply concerns. It is predicted that the country will attain an annual production capacity of 18.3 million tons by 2010, almost triple last year's 9.67 million ton capacity, while China's annual demand for petrochemical products is forecasted to reach 25.5 million tons by the same time.

The Middle Eastern region has great leverage in the production of petrochemical products such as polyethylene due to its abundant feedstocks and low production costs. Ethane, the raw material used to produce polyethylene, only costs around $37 to $50 a ton to produce in the region, one-fifth of its price on the international market.

The Middle East is expected to have 13.8 million tons of polyethylene for export annually by 2010, and China's coastal regions are the main target, according to Liu.

Sun Yanyan, from the chemical department of China Petroleum & Chemical Corp. (Sinopec), noted that six countries in the Gulf Region have been lobbying China's Ministry of Commerce to further reduce petrochemical import tariffs.

"Negotiations have been going on for a year so far, and if the lower tariffs are successfully realized, then import volumes into the country will be boosted," Zhang said.

She added that Sinopec will run their newly upgraded and expanded refineries at full capacity, and will only consider production cutbacks if ample evidence is shown that the Chinese market is unable to consume all the petrochemical products available.

If oversupply of petrochemical products does occur in the Chinese market, Hu Chunli from the Industrial Economic Research Institute under the National Development and Research Commission, believes that the government will step in to help regulate the market at the macro level.

"The Chinese government has already restricted foreign investment in petrochemical products that are already at oversupply levels or which have posed such a trend," Hu said.

Jiang Xianfeng, a Nanjing-based petrochemical product trader, is optimistic that supply shortfalls will remain, especially for basic petrochemical products, due to China's continued rapid economic growth. There is some support for this position, as in 2020, China's GDP is expected to be four times that of its 2000 figure, according to Qin Weizhong, vice director of Sinopec's development and planning department.

However, Jiang predicted tough times are ahead for petrochemical exporters that have traditionally served the Chinese market, such as those in neighboring Japan, Korea and the Taiwan region. "Their import volume to China is likely to be replaced by producers from the Middle East," Jiang said.

However, Tadashi Sudo, general manager of Japan's Sumitomo Chemical Corp., said that exporting petrochemical products directly from Japan has been an overly expensive in practice for a long time now due to high production costs. For this reason, the company has been supplying the Chinese market through its production plant in Singapore.

"We are also considering investing in certain Middle Eastern refineries and petrochemical plants in order to take advantage of their cheap and abundant feedstocks," Sudo said.

"Maybe someday in the future, China will take in cheap imports from the Middle East, while exporting their own output to neighboring countries with higher domestic production costs such as Japan and Korea," Sudo added.

Sample 10 (2)

The Pros and Cons of the Hong Kong Cyberport Project

As the Hong Kong SAR emerged from the Asian recession in March 1999, the Financial Secretary Sir Donald Tsang announced two landmark developments pointing towards Hong Kong's 21st century: Disneyland on Lantau Island, and the "Cyberport" at Pokfulam. The Cyberport project seemed to give a clear signal that Hong Kong was at last poised to take a leading role in the emerging sector of e-commerce and IT.

However, the Cyberport development has been criticized from a number of angles. Some commentators have suggested that it is little more than a residential development with an IT tag (Webb, 1999). The absence of a tender process for the deal seemed to indicate an absence of free competition. Questions were also raised as to whether it is in any case appropriate to create a building to house IT firms "under one roof". Local broadband capability is already powerful, enabling instantaneous communication around the territory.

In this essay, I would like to take a short but critical look at the Cyberport project. Is it a sensible strategic investment? Or is it simply another Hong Kong residential development pretending to be a high-tech miracle?

How can we define the term "Cyberport"? It exists, as yet, in no dictionary, so what follows is tentative: "Cyber" is clearly borrowed from cyberspace, the buzzword of the new millennium. "Port" implies a place where traffic enters (fittingly enough the development is to be built in Telegraph Bay, where the first submarine telegraph came onshore last century). It also arguably suggests "portal", a place where the Internet can be accessed.

According to the government there is a rationale behind the project:

"The Cyberport will create a strategic cluster of IT and information services companies and a critical mass of professional talents. It will act as a focal point for these like-minded companies and professionals to exchange ideas, expertise and unleash creative synergy. And benefits will flow through to the whole community." (Hong Kong Government, 12, 1999).

The use of phrases such as "strategic cluster" and "critical mass" suggests that companies will benefit from being physically close to one another. This is, to say the least, an irony in an age of instantaneous broadband communication and online video conferencing. The whole point of such technology is to make it unnecessary to work in the same place.

What are the other perceived benefits of the Cyberport? Again—according to the government—the concrete benefits include stimulus to the "high value added services" end of the economy, job creation, the development of a multimedia production industry, and (somewhat hopefully perhaps) creation of a new tourist attraction. It will also, however, require the initial import of a highly skilled workforce, then a transfer of skills to local personnel, which should encourage local youth to "excel in IT". Many leading companies have indeed signed letters of intent to buy space in the Cyberport and its success seems assured. (Hong Kong Government, 4, 1999).

However, what would happen if the government had not gone ahead with this expensive venture? Would the IT sector have suffered? It is possible that Hong Kong would have lost out further to Singapore and other countries where the government is taking a positive attitude to the construction of business parks. It is also probable that the realignment of the Hong Kong business community to embrace IT and e-commerce companies would also have developed very much more slowly that it has.

Is the Cyberport really necessary, or is it simply window dressing; good public relations for the government and (with its high residential element) a sound traditional property development? (Webb, 1999)

In terms of IT infrastructure Hong Kong already has a fully digital telephone system and fiber optic lines covering most of the territory. International bandwidth is also wide and growing. In numerous modern office blocks, you can get as much bandwidth as you want—for example the new developments such as "The Centre" or the "Cheung Kong Centre". Any IT business which needs modern offices, reliable power supplies and high-speed data lines can have it now! So in terms of office provision, the Cyberport offers nothing that cannot be found already in Hong Kong.

If the Cyberport building is not necessary, how could the government go about encouraging IT development in Hong Kong? As has been noted by various sources in the existing IT sector, Hong Kong education is at present not producing graduates with the caliber and flexibility to adapt to rapidly changing environments. (Lynch, 1999). One of the ironies of the new Cyberport project is that a "critical mass" of skilled workers will have to be imported to make the project attractive to international companies. The critical problem for Hong Kong right now is how to upgrade the educational institutions so that they start providing useful graduates for the 21st century.

Is the Cyberport project going to be good news for Hong Kong? It could be argued that it has served a very useful purpose on the public relations front: The Hong Kong IT sector is now firmly on the international map and companies in the sector are now attracting attention from the international financial community. The government has been seen to act decisively and with commitment to the SAR's economic future at a time when the economic outlook looked none too bright. Even the way in which the contract was awarded—though criticized by many at the time as an example of unfair business practice (the contract was not put out to competitive tender) attracted enormous international attention and, it could be argued, helped to raise the international profile of the project!

It can safely be concluded that whereas the Cyberport may not be a practical necessity for IT companies who wish to relocate to Hong Kong, it has already been beneficial in raising the profile of the local IT sector. Whether it will now go on to make a concrete contribution to the economy remains to be seen. But all the early signs look hopeful. Hong Kong has for long been perceived as a place where property prices and finance are the "core" businesses. For the future, IT and e-commerce will now stand a chance of being as centrally placed in Hong Kong as in the other advanced economies of the world.

Sample 10 (3)

Thailand, China Sign WTO Deal

China and Thailand clinched a bilateral trade agreement on China's entry into the World Trade Organization (WTO) yesterday in Beijing, removing another obstacle to China's 14-year pursuit of membership of the global trade body.

"The agreement not only is testimony to our long-standing relationship but signals the emergence of China's economy as part of the world economy," Thai Deputy Prime Minister Supachai Panitchpakdi said after signing the agreement with Chinese Minister of Foreign Trade and Economic Co-operation Shi Guangsheng.

The accord reduced to 11 the number of countries or trading blocs with which China has yet to conclude negotiations on WTO entry.

Shi told reporters after the signing ceremony that he was expecting to meet the European Union (EU) Foreign Trade Commissioner Pascal Lamy in the last week of this month to conclude the Sino-EU bilateral WTO negotiation.

The EU is by far the largest of China's partners who have yet to conclude a bilateral trade deal necessary for China to enter the WTO.

"After the two rounds of talks in Brussels and Beijing, we have made important progress," Shi said.

He said he was full of confidence that the two trade partners could find a way that both sides could accept in the forthcoming negotiation.

China has seen its WTO negotiation process remarkably accelerated after it hammered out a landmark agreement with the United States in November last year.

Apart from Thailand, China also wrapped up a trade deal with India in Beijing in late February and completed WTO talks with Colombia on Tuesday in Bogota.

"We have entered the final phase for bilateral WTO negotiations and it won't be long before China's final accession to the WTO," Shi said.

Supachai said he strongly supported China's entry into the WTO before the initiation of the new round of WTO negotiations.

"It is indeed significant that China might become a member before a new round is launched," he said.

"China's membership of WTO will bring about more equality in the allocation of resources between WTO member countries," he added.

Supachai is scheduled to take over from Mike Moore as WTO director general in 2002, as part of a deal ending months of bitter leadership battles that carved deep divides in the world trade body.

Shi said China could co-operate well with other WTO members and support the work of the WTO Secretariat after it formally joined the international trade group.

"China will play a positive and constructive role in the next round of multilateral negotiations," he said.

Sample 10 (4)

High-tech Boards to Open Soon

China's planned high-tech boards on its securities market—the equity market which is similar to the Growth Enterprises Market (GEM) in Hong Kong—are expected to be launched on June 1 in Shanghai and Shenzhen Stock Exchanges, according to sources close to the top securities regulators.

Over 70 high-tech firms have already been granted approval for the new market by the top regulating authorities—the Chinese Securities Regulatory Commission (CSRC)—including a number of Shanghai-based technology firms, said Fan Yongjin, president of the Shanghai Asset Reshuffling Leading Group Office for the Local Listed Firms.

The office is now in charge of recommending and selecting qualified local high-tech firms that intend to seek funds from the planned equity market.

"The total number of those would-be listed firms could be extended to 200 to 300 during the first stage of the boards," said Fan.

A hefty increase in numbers is likely as the boards continue to expand and more firms emerge on the home market.

Rumors prevailed in the market that there are still over 1,000 firms waiting for evaluation by the Ministry of Science and Technology and the Chinese Academy of Science—two of the major watchdogs that are authorized to grant the title of high-tech firms.

And only those firms that successfully pass the appraisal of these two institutions can apply for listing on the boards.

China has made repeated calls for the development of the country's high-tech companies, which largely enjoy favorable taxation conditions but face tough funding shortfalls.

To ease the problem of financing the growth of these firms, the State has adopted many favorable policies to stimulate the industry, including the launch of State-backed venture capitals, the introduction of foreign venture capitals and the inauguration of the high-tech boards at Shanghai and Shenzhen Stock Exchanges.

And the government has also promised to minimize the qualifications for the high-tech companies that intend to be listed on the boards, according to Fan.

Technology companies aiming to list on the new boards must first have a minimal two-year-long history and record profits for one year, compared with three years of profits for other firms seeking listing on the main board.

And the minimum registered capital for the high-tech board firms has also been reduced to 30 million yuan (US $3.62 million), compared with that of 50 million (US $6.04 million) for other firms.

Sample 10 (5)

Overseas Markets Offer More Opportunities

The outlook for the building materials industry in China is improving, Huang Jinfeng of the State Administration of Building Materials Industry said.

"Demand from Asian countries outside China, a traditional market for China's building materials, is improving. Their economies are recovering from the financial crisis," said Huang, director of the administration's foreign affairs department.

Chinese entrepreneurs' growing awareness of the need to "go outward" because of China's possible accession to the World Trade Organization will help increase exports, she said.

"Relevant departments have decided to return value-added taxes paid when enterprises export high-tech building materials products beginning this year," she said.

"We are talking with the State Economic and Trade Commission about returning value-added taxes for deep-processed products."

"We are planning to provide financial services for exports of building materials technologies and equipment," Huang said.

According to Huang, China will hold a building materials exhibition in the Netherlands during the first half of this year to explore European markets.

The time is ripe for us to increase exports to these countries, because the quality of our building materials is adequate to meet the demand, she said.

"We plan to export US$2.5 billion worth of building materials in 2000," she said.

China's building materials exports grew steadily in 1999 after a recession stemming from the Asian financial crisis in 1997, according to a report from the administration's information office.

Exports were valued at US$2.32 billion in 1999, up 6.02 percent from 1998.

Major exports were glass fibre products, sanitary ceramics and asbestos products, the report said.

More than 70 percent of export income was from Japan, Belgium and the United States, the report said.

China imported US$1.57 billion worth of building materials in 1999, up 28.9 percent, "the majority of which Chinese factories could not produce," Huang said.

10.5 NOTES

(1) feedstock: the raw material that is required for some industrial process （送入机器或加工厂的）原料
(2) the pros and cons 赞成和反对的论据、票数
(3) cyberport: a place where you can buy digital machines 数码港
(4) hierarchical: classified according to various criteria into successive levels or layers 分层的；等级（制度）的

10.6 COMMUNICATION LABORATORY

A. Give a brief answer to the following questions.
  (1) What are articles usually written for?
  (2) What techniques can you use to make your articles coherent?

B. Case Study

You work for Oriental Furniture Co. Your company has recently made an arrangement with a local sports center for employees of the company to use their facilities free of charge. Write an article for your company's weekly magazine to encourage other employees to use these facilities.

Unit 11　Business Advertisments

Advertisements are all around us today. They permeate every section of the society and especially in business. Advertising is widely used in marketing for it can persuade potential customers to buy the advertised.

AMA(American Marketing Association) defines advertisement as "the non-personal communication of information usually paid for and usually persuasive in nature about products, services or ideas by identified sponsors through the various media". In other words, the sponsor of an advertisement pays for it to get across to the public some information about the advertised.

The aim of an advertisement is to gain the reader's attention of the advertised, to convince him of its superiority and motivate him to take the action of purchase.

11.1　CATEGORIES OF ADVERTISEMENTS

Based on the different kinds of the advertised, advertisements can be classified into: Product Advertisements, Service Advertisements, Job Advertisements and Business Advertisements. A product advertisement introduces a product to consumers and to persuade them to buy it. A service advertisement is also to promote a product. However, in this case the product promoted is intangible service. The aim of a job advertisement is to find talents for enterprises. A business advertisement is actually an introduction to an enterprise, in which its business line, main products or services and some other important information are described to establish its profile.

Advertisements can also be typed in their different media. They can be carried through the medium of newspapers, magazines, radio, TV, letters or posters. Owing to its popularity, newspaper is an important medium for advertising. Compared with advertisements through other media, newspaper advertisement has advantages in its broad reach, geographical selectivity, flexibility, and immediacy. Magazine, also an important medium for advertising, is powerful in its selectivity, high quality of reproduction, long life, believability and pass-along readership. The main advantage of radio advertisement is the low cost. Besides, it can convey information to the targeted people quickly. TV advertisement is now the most popular kind of advertisements. It has mass coverage, great impact, high prestige and flexibility. Direct mail advertisement is flexible in its format, easy to control and high in response rate. Advertisements on billboard or painted display, posters or neon signs fall into the category of outdoor advertisements. These advertisements are low in cost per message, wide in coverage and high in reach and frequency.

In practice, advertisements of different kinds of goods are carried through different media. For example, those goods for daily use are often advertised on TV or radio.

In this unit the advertisements in magazines and newspapers are to be discussed.

11.2 COMPONENTS OF ADVERTISEMENT COPY

An advertisement copy usually consists of six components: Headline, Lead-in, Body, Slogan, Supplementary Items, and Illustration.

11.2.1 Headline

The headline of an advertisement, usually in a form of short paragraph or some phrases, highlights the topic of the advertisement. It is in fact a key component of an advertisement, for five times as many people read the headline as read the body copy.

An effective headline should reach out to the reader with what is of interest to him, and so attracts the selected target. For example, the headline of a shedding tool "Remove Hair Forever" may catch the eye of those who want to molt. Headlines should also motivate the reader to read on by using words that can arouse the reader's curiosity. The headline of an advertisement for a small hotel "the mouse that roared" is just a case in point. Besides, a headline should include the name of trademark if possible.

Sometimes the headline of an advertisement can be written in the form of a title plus a subtitle. For instance, the headline for "Seals Tyre" is

> This is Seals' New Self-sealing Tyre
> You Could Drive It with a Dozen Nails in It

11.2.2 Lead-in

The lead-in of an advertisement is the section between the headline and the body copy. But it is not a mere shifting from headline to the body copy; it is a summing-up of the whole body. A good lead-in should enable the reader to catch the main idea of the advertisement. Take for an example an advertisement for *China Daily*: "China's only English-language newspaper, offers readers both at home and abroad China's latest political, economic, cultural, educational and other developments".

11.2.3 Body

The main section of an advertisement is the body. It is in this section to fulfill the task of persuading the reader to take action. The following is an advertisement for a park:

> There is so much to see and do for all ages and it's all in the perfect setting of Xiamen's finest landscaped gardens.

> Beautiful flowers and plants, meadows and playgrounds, trees with picnic areas ... plus tea rooms, snack bars, souvenir shops ... the park brings you immense leisure and recreation. A new Tropical Aquarium within the grounds adds to the special features of the park.
>
> With the incredibly cheap admission charges of 5 yuan for adults, 2 yuan for children, and free for retired aged citizens, it really is the perfect day out in Jinshan Park!

This body, which explains clearly the benefits of visiting the park, can surely draw visitors there.

The body of advertisement falls into four categories: straight-line copy, narrative copy, testimonial copy and descriptive copy.

In a straight-line copy, the merits of the advertised are illustrated with facts. This kind of copy is used mainly in the advertisements for goods like equipments or goods with sophisticated structures, which are popular for its uniqueness. The following body of an advertisement for Toshiba Copier is a straight-line copy:

> **Feel the Power of the World's First Turbo Copier**
> Introducing the new Toshiba 2230 Turbo. The first turbocharged copier in history.
> Beneath its sleek exterior is a copying system. So remarkable it's actually patented.
> With it, you can produce 22 copies a minute. Or hit the turbo button and turn out 30 copies a minute. So now you have the power to work 40% more efficiently. While using 33% less toner. And what's even more revolutionary, we've managed to do it all without turbo charging the price.
> To arrange for a free demonstration, just call 1-800-Go-Toshiba.

The body of an advertisement which is written in the style of daily conversation is a narrative copy. This kind of body is persuasive in that it may arouse confidence in the reader with its natural language. The following is an example of this kind of body.

> Everyone is born with fat feet; and extra padding of fatty tissue that cushions footstep. But as we grow older, we lose that tissue until there's little left to absorb the bumps and jolts.
>
> That's why your feet get tired and sore. Dr. Sholl's AirtDille Insoles help take the place of that fatty tissue. They are soft, so you'll feel comfortable difference with every step. They are thin, so slip into your shoes without bunching and binding. As they help keep feet cooler and drier.
>
> Because the older your feet get, the more you have to baby them.

Sometimes the body of advertisement is written in the form of testimony. In this kind of advertisements, some authorities are quoted praising the advertised. For example,

> ... As Mr. Stiles recalls: One ad said that a Volvo was so tough, you could "Drive it like you hate it". I did exactly that. In my field work I've driven this car 295,000 hard miles, much of it through former Indian territory. It's held up even better than promised. Driving it like I hated it made me love it ...

Some advertisements are written by means of description. Take for example an advertisement for Thai Airline,

> Fly smooth as silk and enjoy award winning food and service. Smooth as silk as an attitude born of a century old culture. It's the natural charm of our cabin and ground crews it's a fresh orchid for every passenger. Smooth as silk is Thai.

Whichever kind of copy is adopted in an advertisement, it should be interesting to read and convincing.

11.2.4 Slogan

Slogan functions as continuity for an advertisement campaign, aiming to strengthen the impression on the reader and arouse in him the desire to buy the advertised. Written in simple words, slogans are concise and easy to memorize. Placed at the end of a copy, a good slogan can help to convince the customers of the necessity of taking action. For example,

> Let's do it better. (Philips)
> A world of comfort. (Japan Airline)
> Just do it. (Nike)
> Fresh-up with Seven-Up. (Seven-Up)
> Quality never goes out of style. (Levi's)

11.2.5 Supplementary Items

This section is a supplement to the body of an advertisement. It usually consists of the trademark, name of the commodity, company logo, address and telephone number of the company, etc. The following is the supplementary items of an advertisement for an electronic body-weighing scale:

> To learn more about PUS-180 electronic body-weighing scale, please tell us your contact way.
> Tel.: 0086-020-64888699
> Fax: 0086-020-64888677
> E-mail: phinx@public.net

11.2.6 Illustration

Illustration is an important visual component of an advertisement, and helps to enhance the persuasiveness of the body. Good illustration can fulfill many functions. it can capture the attention of the reader, and help him identify the subject of the advertisement. Besides, it can arouse interest in the reader for him to read on, create him a favorable impression and help clarify claims made in the copy and convince him of the truth of these claims.

11.3 ENGLISH IN ADVERTISING

English in advertising has its own features in morphology, syntax, and rhetorical devices.

11.3.1 Morphology in Advertising

To make it easy for the reader to understand the copy, simple, colloquial and commendatory words are used in advertisements. For example, the advertiser of "Dove" soap changed the original version "Dove makes soap obsolete" to "Dove makes soap old-fashioned", for "obsolete" is not a word commonly used.

There are 20 verbs that are thought to be most commonly used in advertisements: like, use, make, take, feel, taste, look, see, go, come, think, try, get, buy, sell, say, enjoy, send, do, and save. These are all monosyllable words that are familiar to almost everyone. So are the 20 most commonly used adjectives in advertisements: new, good, fine, comfortable, well, lasting, fast, efficient, superb, top, up-to-date, hot, warm, cool, easy, convenient, young, healthy, clean, and safe. All these words are common and commendatory words.

Another feature in the diction of advertisements is the wide use of compounds. Take for example the following compounds in advertisements: top-quality bulbs, piping-hot coffee, cost-effective copier, and relief-giving liquid. Furthermore, in advertisements a lot of vivid and striking new compounds are created. The following are some examples of this kind of compounds:

> (1) Our newest design is made of rain-and-stain-resisting cloth.
> (2) American Express—do it right, first-rate, top-notch, without a hitch and absolutely flawless.
> (3) Even if just over $100 per person per day, our thrill-of-a-life trips are cheap.
> (4) Our bank offers advantages-tailored service.

Besides in English advertisements there are lots of loan words and coinages. Loan words can help to impress the reader, for they can add to some glamour or color of the advertised. For example, advertisements for food and restaurants often make use of French words.

> (5) We have the *Chef* from Paris.
> (6) Perrier ... with added *je ne sais quoi*.

In Example (5) the French word "chef" is used instead of the English word "cook", for France is famous for its cuisine. In Example (6) the French terms "je ne sais quo", meaning "I don't know what", may add to the curiosity of the reader.

Advertisers often coin words to bring about refreshing imagination. For example, the coin word "Orangemostest" in the advertisement for a drink "The Orangemostest Drink in the world" is the combination of "orange", "most" and "est". Some words in advertisements are deliberately misspelled to make it more vivid, interesting and appealing. A case in point is "Drinka pinta Milka day", a misspelled version of "Drink a pint of milk a day", which makes clever use of the pronunciation of "of".

In addition, two words "we" and "you" are widely used in advertisements to make the reader feel that the manufacturer takes into account the consumers' interests. Take for example an advertisement for watch: "We made this watch for you—to be part of your life—simply because this is the way we've always made watches."

"I" tone is also often used to draw the reader to the copy, for it not only sounds more convincing, but also makes customer feel that what is said worth trusting as the storyteller is one of them. The effectiveness of this tone can be shown in the advertisement for a kind of bulb: "I've replaced 1,453 diapers, and 18 baby-sitters, but never the bulb since I became a dad two years ago."

11.3.2 Syntax in English Advertising

Advertisement English, like other styles of English, has its own characteristics in syntax.

One of the striking features is that there are many simple sentences in advertisements. Advertisers use simple sentences in consideration of the fact that it is easy for the reader to catch the meaning of simple sentences, while it is likely to get bored to read long complicated sentences. For instance, all the sentences are simple in an advertisement of the Coca-Cola Company: "Your needs have changed. Your tastes have changed. And the Coca-Cola Company is changing along with you."

Another characteristic of advertisement English is the wide use of elliptical sentence. For example,

> (1) Born to run. (car)
> (2) The hotel best facilitated and full entertainment service. (hotel)
> (3) More than a timepiece. An acquisition. (watch)
> (4) A mild way. Make it a Mild Smoke. Smooth, rich, rewarding. (cigarette)

In addition, interrogative sentences and imperative sentences are often found in advertisement English. It is said that in advertisements there is an interrogative sentence every thirty sentences. The main function of interrogative sentence is to arouse questions in the reader and thus attract him to read on. For example,

> (5) What kind of men reads *Playboy*? He's a man who demands ... (magazine)
> (6) What difference does it make that Lufthansa flier to more international destinations than any other single airline? (airline)

(7) What is the chance to win cold cash with your hot coffee? A piece of dough with your donut? A full two grand with your full tank? (gas station)

(8) What will you do with the money you save using faster, more efficient computer? (computer)

Imperative sentences are common in advertisements for the reason that they imply demands and requests, which coincides with the purpose of advertisements. For example,

(9) Step in a store near you. Take a look. Go ahead, compare. See for yourself. Visit an authorized IBM Personal Computer dealer. (computer)

(10) Put it all behind you. (car)

(11) Look for Top Shelf on your grocer's shelf in the new microware entrée section, and go places with it. (food)

(12) Get ready to encounter the new trend in timepieces.
The Citizen Extreme Collection.
Watch that are indicators of tastes and moods, that express you.
(watch)

Advertising English is unique also in that many sentences are split on purpose. This is aimed to enlarge the amount of information through splitting a sentence into more information fragments, which usually highlights the specifics the advertiser wants to emphasize. For example,

(13) Italian wines. The quality of life. (wine)

(14) Konica film cameras. The power of purity. (camera)

(15) ... colors that look lastingly tempting. Longer. (paint)

(16) ... Italy's masterpiece. A delightful liqueur created from wild hazelnuts, herbs and berries.
Ah!
Frangelico. (drink)

11.3.3 Rhetorical Devices in English Advertising

English advertisements are rich in its use of rhetorical devices. Repetition, simile or metaphor, personification, parallelism, contrast, pun, alliteration or end rhyme, hyperbole are the most commonly used rhetorical devices in advertisements.

Repetition is used in advertisements for emphasis. For example,

(1) *Free* Hotel! *Free* Meals! *Free* Transfer! For a *Free* "stay-on-the-way" in Amsterdam. (hotel)

(2) You can't *Xerox* a *Xerox* on a *Xerox*. (copier)

(3) When *you're sipping* Lipton, *you're sipping* something special.

> (4) *I don't know* who you are.
> *I don't know* your company.
> *I don't know* your company's product.
> *I don't know* what your company stands for.
> *I don't know* your company's customers.
> *I don't know* your company's record.
> *I don't know* your company's reputation.
> Now what is it you wanted to tell me?
> Moral: Sales start before your salesman calls—with business publication advertising. (magazine)

Similes and metaphors are both widely used in English advertising to create vivid images. For example,

> (5) Fly smooth as silk and enjoy award-winning food and service. (airline)
> (6) Pick an Ace from Toshiba. (computer)
> (7) The most sensational place to wear satin is on your lips. (lipstick)
> (8) Go for the Gold.
> Goldstar.
> The brightest star in electronics. (electronics)

Personification is another rhetorical device used in English advertising:

> (9) Unlike me, my Rolex never needs a rest. (watch)
> (10) Even cold rolled steel can have a heart and soul. (car)
> (11) Flowers by Interflora speak from the heart. (flower shop)
> (12) We are proud of the birthplaces of our children, the grapes of Almaden.
> On our classic varietal wines, you will find the birthplaces of our children. (wine)

Parallelism is also widely used in advertising:

> (13) Wherever you are. Whatever you do. The Allianze Group Insurance Company is always on your side. (insurance)
> (14) Diamonds for modern women. For me, for now, for ever. (diamond)
> (15) More space means more options. (truck)
> (16) ... It is made differently. It is made using skills and techniques that others have lost or forgotten. It is made with attention to detail very few people would notice. It is made, we have to admit, with a total disregard for time ... (electronics)

Contrast is used in advertising to highlight the advertised.

130 A Practical Coursebook for Business English Writing

> (17) Tide's in, dirt's out. (washing powder)
> (18) Mini size, Maxi sound. (stereo)
> (19) No problem too large. No business too small. (IBM)
> (20) It's e-business or out of business. (computer)

Advertisers make use of pun to create associations.

> (21) I am More satisfied. ("More" cigarette)
> (22) Make Time for Time. (*Time* magazine)
> (23) From sharp minds. Come Sharp products. ("Sharp" electronics)
> (24) The label of achievement. Black Label commands more respect. ("Black Label" whisky)

Both alliteration and end rhyme are used in advertisements to make the copy sound better.

> (25) We place the power in your hands. Safe, Secure, Confidential. (scanner)
> (26) Smooth, satisfy taste at ultra-low tar. (cigarette)
> (27) A smooth silky skin. (cosmetics)
> (28) A simple solution for a healthy home. (detergent)
> (29) Get three. The fourth is free. (book)
> (30) From ships to Chips. (Hyundai Corporation)
> (31) Let the "kitchen maid" be your kitchen aid. (cupboard)
> (32) Go for the sun and fun. (travel)

Another rhetorical device that is widely used in English advertisements is hyperbole.

> (33) The world is shrinking. (magazine)
> (34) Take Toshiba, take the world. (electronics)
> (35) The only thing we didn't improve was the road. (car)
> (36) The only sound you'll hear is praise. (car)

11.4 SAMPLE ADVERTISEMENTS

Sample 11 (1)

> **Woodbury's Facial Soap**
> A skin you love to touch ... Your skin, as it is now, is not a lifetime possession by any means. If you have thought so, you have overlooked this big fact: Your skin, like the rest of your body, is changing every day. As old skin dies, new forms. This is your opportunity. By the proper external treatment, you can make this new skin just what you would love to have it. Write today for this picture! See offer below.

Sample 11（2）

> ### Imagine What a Cannon Color Laser Copier
> ### Could Do with a Pie Chart
>
> *The Cannon Color Laser Copier 200 could do a lot for your business. And Digital Image Processing is the reason.*
>
> Now copiers from graphics, slides and photos look more life-like while text stays pure black. Reproductions comparable to professional printing with 256 gradations per color and 400 dots per inch resolution. And with 50% to 400% zoom and advanced editing, as well as automatic feeding and sorting functions and a quick 20 black-and-white copies per minute. It's one color copier, that's all business.
>
> To find out more, call 1-800-OK-CANON, or write us at
> Canon USA Inc., P. O. Box 3900, Peoria, II, 61614,
> Canon Color Laser Copier the Digital Difference

Sample 11（3）

> ### A Unique Collectors
> ### Watch by Patek Philippe
>
> *Only twenty will ever be made*
>
> Boodle & Dunthorne are privileged to be the first
> ever to commission Patek Philippe to create a limited
> edition watch of such importance.
> Cased in platinum, it has a timeless elegance that
> will never date. Each boasts a perpetual calendar
> movement to indicate the day, date and month as
> well as marking the hour, minute and second.
> **It is a fine watch, a very fine watch indeed. A watch
> for the most discerning collector.**

Sample 11（4）

> ### Over 200 Years of Careful Breeding
> ### Produced This Champion
>
> Every once in a while, a truly great horse is born. A horse destined to become a supreme champion on the race course and to pass to the legend. A Ninjinsky or an Aride, a Red Rum or a Shirgar—superb animals who remain unchallenged in their lifetimes.
>
> But perfection does not come about by chance. Such a horse is the result of the careful breeding of the bluest of bloodlines that can be traced for generations. And from the day of its birth, the young horse will be lovingly nurtured and cared for, meticulously shaped into a champion.
>
> So it is with Hine X. O., the champion of fine cognacs, the choice of connoisseurs.

132　A Practical Coursebook for Business English Writing

> Established in the heart of the Cognac region of France in 1763, the house of Hine has remained unswervingly faithful to the standards of quality set down by its founder, Thomas Hine.
>
> Since the eighteenth century, every drop of Hine cognac has been lovingly matured under the watchful eye of one man, the cell master, whose senses are his birthright and whose extraordinary talents can be traced back through six generations of the Hine family.
>
> Hine X. O. —a thorough bred champion of maturity, delicacy and finesse. A cognac of incomparable quality, to be savored with respect and infinite pleasure.
>
> Hine leaves nothing to be desired.

Sample 11（5）

> In-depth coverage of the news making headlines across the nation.
Stay connected. Stay informed. Subscribe today.
Discover the benefits of becoming a subscriber.
Here are some highlights of the benefits you get by subscribing to USA TODAY.
>
> **Unlimited access to national news.**
> As a member, you get in-depth coverage and unlimited access to the national news that matters most to you. USA TODAY's commitment to the public good through great journalism never wavers.
>
> **Easy-to-use apps for direct access to the news you want.**
> Be the first to know about breaking news as it happens and stay connected with your community through our various smartphone and tablet apps. We offer apps based on specific interests and members have access to content that others don't.
>
> **Electronic Edition of the Newspaper.**
> On the go? Take the news with you. You get an exact digital replica of USA TODAY. The enewspaper allows you to flip the pages, scan the headlines, and read the stories on your device of choice, any time.
>
> **Newsletters tailored to your interests.**
> Sign up for our newsletters and get breaking news, weather forecasts, recipes and more. Select the topics you like, and we'll deliver tailored content directly to your inbox.

11.5　NOTES

(1) product advertisements　产品广告
(2) service advertisements　服务广告
(3) job advertisements　招聘广告
(4) business advertisements　业务广告
(5) newspaper advertisements　报纸广告
(6) magazine advertisements　杂志广告
(7) radio advertisements　广播广告

(8) TV advertisements 电视广告

(9) direct mail advertisements 直邮广告

(10) outdoor advertisements 户外广告

(11) broad reach 覆盖率高

(12) geographical selectivity 地区选择性(高)

(13) flexibility 灵活性(强)

(14) immediacy 时间性(强)

(15) selectivity 选择性(强)

(16) high quality of reproduction 复制效果好

(17) long life 寿命长

(18) believability 可信度(高)

(19) pass-along readership 传阅率(高)

(20) mass coverage 覆盖率广

(21) great impact 影响力大

(22) high prestige 声誉高

(23) flexible in its format 形式灵活

(24) easy to control 易于控制

(25) high in response rate 反应率高

(26) subscribe 预订；订阅(for, to)

(27) breaking news 突发新闻

(28) tablet apps 平板电脑应用

(29) tailor (为某一特定目的)制作

(30) logo 标识

(31) loan words 外来词语

(32) coinage 新造的词语

(33) replica 拷贝；完全一样的事物

(34) digital image processing 数字图像处理

(35) gradation 灰度

(36) 400 dots per inch resolution 分辨率是 400 DPI

(37) automatic feeding 自动进纸

(38) on the go 非常忙碌

(39) bluest of bloodlines 最高贵的出身

(40) meticulously 细致地；过细地

(41) X.O. "extra old"的缩写,指藏窖年份达 40—75 年的白兰地酒

(42) connoisseurs 鉴赏家

(43) unswervingly 坚持不懈地

(44) finesse 手腕；技巧；策略

(45) Hereunder are some useful expressions:

  * above money's worth

* a full range of service
* a completely new experience
* a great variety of
* a unique prescription
* attractive and durable
* bargain sale
* beneficial to all ages
* choice material
* convenient in maintenance
* cordial service
* easy installation
* exclusive brand
* a complete range of specification
* an old established firm
* bright in color
* care free
* comfortable feel
* comprehensive service
* consummate skill
* delicate and exquisite
* dependable quality
* easy operation
* economical and practical
* excellent workmanship
* exquisite craftsmanship
* famed and precious
* fast color
* fresh keeping package
* gladden the eye and heart
* genuine goods and reasonable price
* have a lasting market
* have a well-deserved reputation
* innovative design
* famous trademark
* fashion leading
* favorable price
* fine workmanship
* first class
* graceful and attractive

* guarantee replacement or refund
* in short supply
* large assortment
* never torn or worn
* opening sales
* reliable performance
* safe and handy
* seasonable cuisine
* stand wear and tear
* local specialty
* prestige first
* raged world-wide
* serve hand and foot
* superb
* take the lead
* true to one's name
* unaffected
* unmatched
* unrivalled
* varied assortment
* wider selection
* with net price marked
* warm and wind-proof
* without additive

11.6 COMMUNICATION LABORATORY

A. Give a brief answer to the following questions.

(1) What are the components of an advertisement?

(2) Describe the four types of advertisement body.

(3) How can an advertisement be made appealing to the audience?

(4) Describe the features of advertisement English.

B. Translate the following advertisement into English.

（Only Aim 除垢牙刷能同时从两面为您洁牙）

您看到过一种能从两个角度为您洁牙的牙刷吗？

牙科保健业的重大发明——除垢牙刷——一种特别能高效除垢的牙刷。

Only Aim 有其独特的双面刷毛,从而能达到专业除垢的功效。

既然您明白它为何被称为除垢牙刷,您又怎么还会继续使用旧式牙刷呢？

除垢牙刷,专门除垢的牙刷,专业人士一致认为它安全有效。

C. Case Study

(1) Write an advertisement copy for a smartwear (watch, fitness wristband, blood pressure monictor, bracelet, ring, etc.) that is of interest to you.

(2) Suppose you are the marketing manager of Honda in China. Write an advertisement body copy for a new model of car.

Unit 12 Business Profiles

Business profiles now widely used by corporations are for self-publicizing and business promoting.

12.1 THE LAYOUT OF BUSINESS PROFILES

Business profiles of corporations in different business lines vary in their contents. However, generally speaking, a business profile may begin with some general introduction to the corporation, such as its ownership, business domains and position in the trade. Then comes the section describing the corporation's history, status quo and management structure. Most business profiles end with prospects of the corporation. Some other information, like the operating system, guiding principles, and corporate values, may also be included in a business profile.

Some business profiles have headlines, which fall into two types. One kind of headlines contains only the name of the corporation, such as the one "Toshiba Group INC" in the profile of Toshiba. Other headlines are written in the form of "Brief Introduction to ... ". For example, the headline of Northwest Airline is "Brief Introduction to Northwest Airline".

The section of general introduction usually describes the ownership of the corporation, its business domains, main product or service, and position in the trade. For example,

> Morris Companies Inc. is a holding company whose principle wholly owned subsidiaries include Philip Morris Incorporated, Philip Morris International Inc., Kraft Foods Inc., and Miller Brewing Company. These companies are engaged in manufacture and sale of various consumer products. Another wholly owned subsidiary, Philip Morris Capital Corporation, is engaged in various leasing and investment activities ...

For another example,

> Toshiba, a world leader in high technology, is a diversified manufacturer and marketer of advanced electronic and electrical products, spanning information and communications equipment and systems, Internet-based solutions and services, electronic components and materials, power systems, industrial and social infrastructure systems, and household appliances.

In business profiles, the corporation's history is an important component for those long-established ones. For example, Heinz writes in its profile, "The history of Heinz is rich in goodness and tradition".

In some profiles this section is highlighted through a detailed account of the development of the corporation. The following is an extraction of history description of Toshiba.

1873—1890	First steps taken toward creation of Toshiba
1891—1931	Growth, disaster and reconstruction
1932—1939	Integrated electrical equipment manufacturer formed from merger of Shibaura Engineering Works (heavy electrical machinery) and Tokyo Electric Company (small electrical equipment)
1940—1956	Major government supplier during the war; exports to Southeast Asia begin in postwar period
1957—1972	Revitalization of management and business structures paves way for overseas expansion
1973—1983	Technical capabilities reinforced to realize consistent growth
1984—1999	Name changed to Toshiba; in-house company system promotes swifter decision-making
Since 2000	Creating World's First and World's No.1 products and services to prevail amid global competition and become an even stronger global contender

Description of the status quo of the corporation is the most important component of a business profile. This part usually includes accounts of the scale, management structure and business portfolio of the corporation.

Large corporations often highlight their size in their profiles. For example, Coco Cola in its profile writes, "People around the world invite our beverages into their lives more than 1.3 billion times a day". In the profile of Northwest Airline, the corporation is described as "one of the world's largest airlines with hubs at Detroit, Minneapolis/St. Paul, Memphis, Tokyo and Amsterdam, and approximately 1,400 daily departures".

Sometimes numbers are used in a profile to show the large scale of the corporation, as can be seen in Toshiba's profile:

Employees:	128,697
Shareholders:	270,570
Total Assets:	¥4,727,113 million (US$40,403 million)
Shareholders' Equity:	¥1,002,165 million (US$8,566 million)
Capital:	¥274,926 million (US$2,350 million)

Management structure of the corporation is also an important component of a business profile. Take for example this part in the Toshiba profile:

(As of July 1, 2019)

Now many corporations cover a wide range of trades, which is illustrated in the part of business portfolio. For example, in the profile of General Electrical, this part is emphasized:

> From jet engines to power generation, financial services to plastics, and medical imaging to news and information, GE people worldwide are dedicated to turning imaginative ideas into leading products and services that help solve some of the world's toughest problems.
>
> GE is made up of six businesses, each of which includes a number of units aligned for growth.
>
> **GE Industrial**
>
> GE Industrial provides a broad range of products and services throughout the world, including appliances, lighting and industrial products; factory automation systems; plastics, silicones and quartz products; security and sensors technology, and equipment financing, management and operating services.
>
> **GE Commercial Finance**
>
> GE Commercial Finance offers an array of services and products aimed at enabling business worldwide to grow. GE Commercial Finance provides loans, operating leases, financing programs, commercial insurance and reinsurance, and other services.
>
> **GE Infrastructure**
>
> GE Infrastructure is one of the world's leading providers of fundamental technologies to developed and developing countries, including aircraft engine, energy, oil and gas, rail and water process technologies and services. GE Infrastructure also provides aviation and energy leasing and financing services.
>
> **GE Healthcare**
>
> GE Healthcare provides transformational medical technologies and services that are shaping a new age of patient care. Our broad range of products, service and expertise in medical imaging and information technologies, medical diagnostics, patient monitoring systems, performance improvement, drug discovery, and biopharmaceutical manufacturing technologies is helping clinicians around the world re-imagine new ways to better diagnose and treat cancer, heart disease, neurological diseases and other conditions earlier.
>
> **GE Money**
>
> GE Money, formerly known as GE Consumer Finance, is a leading provider of credit services to consumers, retailers, auto dealers and mortgage lenders across 50 countries worldwide, offering financial products such as credit cards, personal loans, mortgage and motor solutions, corporate travel and purchasing cards as well as debt consolidation and home equity loans.
>
> **GE Universal**
>
> NBC Universal is one of the world's leading media and entertainment companies in the development, production and marketing of entertainment, news and information to a global audience.

Another component that is often found in business profiles is corporate value, which is now attracting more and more attention. Take for example the sections in the profiles of Toshiba and General Electrical.

Toshiba

We, the Toshiba Group companies, based on our total commitment to people and to the future, are determined to help create a higher quality of life for all people, and to do our part to help ensure that progress continues within the world community.

Commitment to People

We endeavor to serve the needs of all people, especially our customers, shareholders, and employees, by implementing forward-looking corporate strategies while carrying out responsible and responsive business activities. As good corporate citizens, we actively contribute to further the goals of society.

Commitment to the Future

By continually developing innovative technologies centering on the fields of Electronics and Energy, we strive to create products and services that enhance human life, and which lead to a thriving, healthy society. We constantly seek new approaches that help realize the goals of the world community, including ways to improve the global environment.

Committed to people, committed to the future. TOSHIBA

General Electric

While GE has always performed with integrity and values, each business generation expresses those values according to the circumstances of the times. Now more than ever the expression and adherence to values is vital.

More than just a set of words, these values embody the spirit of GE at its best. They reflect the energy and spirit of a company that has the solid foundation to lead change as business evolves. And they articulate a code of behavior that guides us through that change with integrity.

They are our words and our values ... in our own voice.

Passionate

Curious

Resourceful

Accountable

Teamwork

Committed

Open

Energizing

Business profiles often end with prospect of the corporation. For example, the profile of Northwest Airline ends as follows:

The Checklist for the Future

Run a Great Airline

Providing safe, clean, on-time air transportation with luggage, in a professional and consistent manner, is the core of Northwest's mission. We provide prompt and appropriate service recovery when, despite our best efforts, something goes wrong. Northwest leads the industry in consistent reliability, a source of competitive success and employee pride.

Put Customers First

Employees have made the Northwest Customers First Plan the industry leader. We have an ongoing commitment through Customers First Plans to continue to outpace our competitors by providing the best customer service in the industry. We will also do our utmost to offer the best service recovery in the industry by solving problems on the spot. We will strive to be the first choice for passengers and shippers with innovative technology and courteous, convenient service. This allows us to create more choices and make it very easy for customers to do business with us, with the best schedules and the simplest access to our network.

Focus on People

By taking care of Northwest people—our greatest asset—they will take care of our customers and our customers will come back in increasing numbers to travel on the Red Tail. We will achieve this objective through enhanced communications, fair and progressive labor relations, state-of-the-art training, and continued improvements to employee services and facilities.

Build Our Network

By expanding service from each Northwest hub, domestically and internationally, by expanding our flying and building our alliances with other carriers we will create robust, profitable and sustainable growth. We will further develop cargo and mail services, enhance sales relationships, and grow capacity by flawlessly executing the long-term fleet plan to take delivery of a new aircraft every two weeks for the next five years.

Secure Our Future

The Company must ensure sustainable financial stability through a commitment to profitability and shareholder value. This is the key to each employee because job security and prosperity are only guaranteed if we are financially successful. To do this we will execute strategies to improve performance, increase productivity, grow revenues, identify high potential areas for expansion, and strengthen our balance sheet by controlling the cost of doing business. We will continue to improve facilities in all service areas and make the investments necessary to execute the checklist. Significant improvements are underway to the terminals and runway systems of all five Northwest hub airports. The best single example of this is the new Northwest World Gateway in Detroit.

12.2 SAMPLE BUSINESS PROFILES

Business profiles vary in their formats. They may be in the format of narratives, format of tables or format of lists.

12.2.1 Narratives

In the narrative type of business profiles, description is used to give unclassified general information of the corporation.

Siemens—Global Network of Innovation

Siemens, headquartered in Berlin and Munich, is one of the world's largest electrical engineering and electronics companies and holds leading market positions in all its business areas. Sustainability for the benefit of its customers, shareholders and employees has been a hallmark of the company ever since its founding 170 years ago. At Siemens, sustainability means long-term economic success coupled with environmental awareness and the social responsibility.

Siemens has a strong international presence, with operations in over 200 countries and manufacturing facilities at about 290 locations worldwide. The company's business portfolio is focused on six key areas: Information and Communications, Automation and Control, Power, Transportation, Medical and Lighting. Global business operations at Siemens are the responsibility of 13 Groups, including Siemens Financial Services and Siemens Real Estate. In addition, Siemens is also a partner in joint ventures—with Bosch in the household appliances sector (BSH Bosch-Siemens Hausgerte) and with Fujitsu in computer systems (Fujitsu Siemens Computers).

The company has a well-balanced business portfolio in the field of electrical engineering and electronics, and its activities are influenced by a variety of regional and sector-specific factors. In addition to internationally oriented businesses, such as Power Generation, Power Transmission and Distribution, Medical Solutions and Transportation Systems, which are generally subject to long-term business cycles, other sectors—for example, the consumer goods businesses in legally separate parts of Information and Communications and Osram, and the capital goods.

12.2.2 Tables

Business profiles in the format of table list the information of the corporation in a table.

Basic Corporate Data

(As of March 31, 2019)

Company Name	Toshiba Corporation
Headquarters Address	1-1, Shibaura 1-chome, Minato-ku, Tokyo, Japan
Founded	July 1875
Chairman and CEO	Nobuaki Kurumatain
President and COO	Satoshi Tsunakawa
Common Stock	¥ 200,044 million
Net Sales (Consolidated Basis)	¥ 3,693.5 billion (FY2018)
Fiscal Year	April 1 to March 31
Number of Employees (Consolidated Basis)	128,697
Number of Shares Issued	544 million shares
Total Number of Shareholders	270,570
Stock Exchange Listings	Japan: Tokyo and Nagoya

12.2.3 Lists

Business profiles may take the form of list. In this kind of profiles information of the corporation is classified.

Exxon Mobil

Exxon Mobil, an industry leader in the energy and petrochemical business.

Our organization structure is built on a concept of global businesses and is designed to allow Exxon Mobil to compete most effectively in the ever-changing and challenging worldwide energy industry.

Exxon Mobil History

The corporate entities that would become Exxon and Mobil began the 20th century as components of one company. At the end of the century, they came together as a single premier organization. For most of the years in between, they blazed separate trails as independent, competing enterprises. Each company placed a singular imprint on the energy industry and on a dynamic era of world history.

Corporate Governance

The Board of Directors of Exxon Mobil Corporation has adopted these corporate governance practices to promote the effective functioning of the Board, its committees and the company. For many years, Exxon Mobil has rigorously adhered to policies and practices that guide the way we do business. The methods we employ to achieve our results are as important as the results themselves. Our corporation expects and requires that its directors, officers and employees observe the highest standards of integrity in the conduct of Exxon Mobil's business.

Activities

Our industry faces an enormous challenge to meet the energy needs of a growing world. Increasingly, significant new oil and gas resources are in more remote areas and difficult operating environments. Major upstream projects are more capital intensive and require substantial financial strength and flexibility. The complexity of the operating environment places greater emphasis on execution excellence. These challenges present Exxon Mobil with opportunities to further differentiate each of our businesses.

Exploration

We explore for oil and natural gas on six of the seven continents. Exxon Mobil's Exploration Company is organized to identify, pursue, capture, and evaluate all high-quality exploration opportunities.

Production

We apply the most cost-effective technology and operations management systems to each and every asset to maximize the commercial recovery of hydrocarbons.

Refining and Supply

We utilize a highly efficient network of manufacturing facilities and transportation and distribution systems to provide clean fuels, lubricants and other high-value products and feedstock to our customers around the world.

Lubricants and Specialties

Anchored by Mobil 1, the world's largest synthetic motor oil, we leverage three strong global brands, Mobil, Exxon and Esso.

Development

Exxon Mobil has a development portfolio of more than 110 projects with potential net investment of more than $120 billion.

Natural Gas and Power Marketing

We sell natural gas in 25 countries and across five continents in most major gas markets in the world.

Fuels Marketing

We sell high-quality products to millions of customers around the globe. Our retails business operates in nearly 100 countries and includes over 35 thousand service stations.

Chemical

Exxon Mobil Chemical is one of the largest worldwide petrochemical companies and is an integrated manufacturer and global marketer of petrochemical products.

Guiding Principles

Exxon Mobil Corporation is committed to being the world's premier petroleum and petrochemical company. To that end, we must continuously achieve superior financial and operating results while adhering to the highest standards of business conduct. These unwavering expectations provide the foundation for our commitments to those with whom we interact:

Shareholders

We are committed to enhancing the long-term value of the investment dollars entrusted to us by our shareholders. By running the business profitably and responsibly we expect our shareholders to be rewarded with superior returns. This commitment drives the management of our company.

Customers

Success depends on our ability to consistently satisfy ever-changing customer preferences. We pledge to be innovative and responsive, while offering high quality products and services at competitive prices.

Employees

The exceptional quality of our workforce is a valuable competitive edge. To build on this advantage we will strive to hire and retain the most qualified people available and maximize their opportunities for success through training and development. We are committed to maintaining a safe work environment enriched by diversity and characterized by open communication, trust, and fair treatment.

Communities

We pledge to be a good corporate citizen in all the places we operate worldwide. We will maintain the highest ethical standards, obey all applicable laws and regulations, and respect local and national cultures. Above all other objectives, we are dedicated to running safe and environmentally responsible operations.

To be successful, Exxon Mobil must be at the leading edge of competition in every aspect of our business. This requires that the Corporation's substantial resources—financial, operational, technological, and human—be employed wisely and evaluated regularly.

> While we maintain flexibility to adapt to changing conditions, the nature of our business requires a focused, long-term approach. We will consistently strive to improve efficiency and productivity through learning, sharing and implementing best practices. We will be disciplined and selective in evaluating the range of capital investment opportunities available to us. We will seek to develop proprietary technologies that provide a competitive edge.
>
> We will achieve our goals by flawlessly executing our business plans and by strictly adhering to these guiding principles along with our more comprehensive standards of business conduct.

12.3 NOTES

(1) status quo 现状

(2) management structure 组织结构

(3) prospects 前景

(4) business domain 业务范围

(5) business portfolio 业务组合

(6) Board of Directors 董事会

(7) Nomination Committee 提名委员会

(8) Compensation Committee 薪资委员会

(9) Audit Committee 审计委员会

(10) capital intensive 资本密集的

(11) state-of-the-art 最先进的

(12) Hereunder are some useful expressions:

* We are ... of long standing and high reputation.
* Our products excel for their workmanship, color, design, and durability.
* The company has won the user's universal trust with products of advanced technology, full functions and reliable qualities.
* Our products have a leading position in the country.
* We are ready to provide excellent service to customers.
* Our products have been highly praised and appreciated by consuming public.
* Our products rank first among similar products.
* Not only are we at the forefront of ... but we've received world-wide recognition for our advances in ... as well.
* Our corporate formula: customers always come first.
* We strive to create products and services that enhance human life, and which lead to a thriving, healthy society.
* ... is a holding company whose wholly owned subsidiaries include ... These companies are engaged in manufacture and sale of various consumer

products.
* ... a world leader in high technology, is a diversified manufacturer and marketer of advanced ...
* Under its mid-term business plan ... is working for enhanced recognition as a highly profitable group of companies, active in both high growth and stable growth businesses.
* Since, ... has been providing people with healthful, nourishing food that is second to none. As we continue to grow, so too grows the scope of our products.
* The history of ... is rich in goodness and tradition. Our community spreads all over the world, with 46,900 employees that share a uniform ... approach: to do a common thing uncommonly well ...
* We ... based on our total commitment to people and to the future, are determined to help create a higher quality of life for all people, and to do our part to help ensure that progress continues within the world community.
* We endeavor to serve the needs of all people, especially our customers, shareholders, and employees, by implementing forward-looking corporate strategies while carrying out responsible and responsive business activities.
* As good corporate citizens, we actively contribute to further the goals of society.
* By continually developing innovative technologies centering on the fields of ..., we strive to create products and services that enhance human life, and which lead to a thriving, healthy society.
* We constantly seek new approaches that help realize the goals of the world community, including ways to improve the global environment.
* We have an ongoing commitment to outpace our competitors by providing the best customer service in the industry.
* We will also do our utmost to offer the best service recovery in the industry by solving problems on the spot.
* We will strive to be the first choice for ... with innovative technology and courteous, convenient service.
* At ... sustainability means long-term economic success coupled with environmental awareness and the social responsibility.
* ... has a strong international presence, with operations in over ... countries and manufacturing facilities at about ... locations worldwide.
* Our organization structure is built on a concept of global businesses and is designed to allow ... to compete most effectively in the ever-changing and challenging worldwide energy industry.

12.4 COMMUNICATION LABORATORY

A. Give a brief answer to the following questions.

(1) What are the components of business profiles?

(2) Describe the features of three types of business profiles.

B. Case Study

国家电网有限公司是根据《公司法》规定设立的中央直接管理的国有独资公司,是关系国民经济命脉和国家能源安全的特大型国有重点骨干企业。公司以投资建设运营电网为核心业务,承担着保障安全、经济、清洁、可持续电力供应的基本使命。

中国电力工业具有 140 年的历史。1949 年中华人民共和国成立后,电力工业管理体制历经多次变化,历经燃料工业部、电力工业部、水电部、能源部,到 1993 年成立电力工业部。1997 年,国家电力公司成立,与电力工业部实

行两块牌子、一套班子运行。2002 年,国务院实施电力体制改革,决定在原国家电力公司部分企事业单位基础上组建国家电网公司。2017 年,国务院实施中央企业公司制改制工作,公司由全民所有制企业整体改制为国有独资公司,名称变更为"国家电网有限公司"。

公司经营区域覆盖 26 个省(自治区、直辖市),覆盖国土面积的 88% 以上,供电服务人口超过 11 亿人。公司注册资本 8295 亿元,资产总额 3.93 万亿元,稳健运营在菲律宾、巴西、葡萄牙、澳大利亚、意大利、希腊等国家和地区的资产。公司连续 14 年获评中央企业业绩考核 A 级企业,位居《财富》世界 500 强前列,是全球最大的公用事业企业。

Unit 13 Resumes and Letters of Application

13.1 RESUMES

A resume is the single document that provides what the applicant believes the most relevant information in presenting to the reader a positive image of himself or herself. It is an important tool in job hunting, applying for a university to study at, putting in for a grant, requesting for a membership at a club, etc.

Unlike a business report which sets to record facts favorable and unfavorable alike with a purpose to offer some insights in decision making or solution formulating, a resume is written primarily for the purpose of convincing the reader by creating a positive image of the resume writer. A successful resume always means an interview or an opportunity which will lead to a success in the benefit the writer is pursuing.

Resumes are normally used together with letters of application, application forms, and letters of recommendation. They can also be used alone as unattached files, with further information or other document sent upon request.

13.1.1 The Layout of Resumes

A resume normally consists of six types of information as is shown in the following list:
- Who is the writer of the resume?
- Where does he/she live?
- How to contact the resume writer?
- What is the objective of the resume?
- What are the qualifications of the resume writer?
- What kind of educational background does the writer have?
- What kind of degree has the writer received?
- What kind of experience does the writer have?
- What kind of honor has the writer of the resume been awarded?
- Does the writer have any references?
- What kind of hobbies or interests the writer may have?

The ways information is organized in resumes are extremely flexible. The six types of information mentioned above should be positioned as shown in the following examples.

Format 1

REUSME

Name: Date of Birth:
Address:
Telephone: E-mail:
Marital Status:
Objective:
Education:
Experience:
Publications:
References:

Format 2

Resume
Alice Standstill

May 13, 2007

Address:
Telephone: **E-mail:**

Experience
2004 – 2007   General Manager of Lancaster Retailing Center

Education
1992 – 1994   Doing postgraduate work at Cambridge College

Qualifications
Proficient in accounting software

Personal Data
Age: **Marital Status:** Single
Hobby: collecting stamps, sports and reading

References

Format 3

Oliver Steinbeck
123 Youth Road, New District, Suzhou 215004

Telephone: **E-mail**:

Job Objective:
Qualifications:
Experience:
Education:
*2005.9 – 2007.6
Certificates:
Reference: Available upon request

Format 4

Toad Eagleton
400 West First Street, Chico, CA 95929-0145

Telephone: **E-mail**:

Job Intention
Manager assistant which will lead to human resources management

Summary of Qualifications
Expert at interpersonal communication; proficient at computer

Management-oriented Education

Degree: **Major**:
Related Courses: **Honor**:

References

Format 1 is an extensive format of resume in which the information is listed one by one in a detailed manner. Format 2 is an intensive format of resume in which the personal information is classified into some general parts. In Format 3, the example is written in the chronological order. In Format 4, the information is organized according to the function of different types of information.

The identifying information like name, mail address, telephone number, fax, and also e-mail address constitutes the heading part of a resume. The name of the applicant occupying a single line can be put in the middle at the top of the page in bold letters serving as a title both to attract the reader and to distinguish the resume from resumes written by other applicants.

The objective of a resume refers to the intention of the applicant. It is the job the applicant is seeking for, the university where the applicant wants to pursue his studies, the organization or club where the applicant wants to be a member, the scholarship or grant the applicant is applying for, etc.

Qualifications are mostly special abilities the applicant has. Information relegated under this part includes one's language proficiency, computer skills, communication capabilities, team spirit, etc. They are just part of what qualifies the applicant for the benefit they are applying for.

The part of education generally contains information about schools where the applicant has received his degrees. The highest degree usually goes first. Basic information about the applicant's education background includes the names of schools, degrees, majors, and any minors if available. Other items to be included are one's experience of further education without degree at home or abroad, and awards or honors achieved in academic field.

The applicant's working experience or other career-related experience constitutes the experience section of a resume. Information about the applicant's working periods, working sites, positions and working achievements should be presented in the reversed chronological order to show the reader what kind of jobs the applicant is capable of and how well the applicant can do these jobs.

References always come last. It customarily contains a single line to show the availability of references, instead of the letters of recommendation proper.

Of course, other types of information can also be included in a resume when necessary. Personal data like interests, hobbies, and social activities often lead to an unexpected result, for they can sometimes arouse a sense of resonance in the reader which means a more favorable response is to be made.

13.1.2 The Planning of Resumes

Resumes follow a direct organization plan in which every piece of information should be presented in a straightforward and direct manner. The steps in organizing a direct-plan resume are: identifying the information to be included in the resume, grouping the information into functional groups, planning the order of the useful data or evidence, and stating the information in a positive response-triggering manner.

Being a document to encourage the receiver to offer the writer an opportunity, the resume should include in it positive information that will convince the receiver of the writer's qualifications.

When planning a resume, the writer should also choose a format or a style that best suits his/her needs.

13.1.3 The Tone of Resumes

Written to stimulate a positive reply, resumes should be conveyed in a persuasive manner. The tone of resumes can range from objective and emotional to subjective. Objectivity conveyed in the message will ensure the receiver that you are presenting your personal data in a faithful and factual manner. Forceful but positive feelings underlying the message will convey your sincerity and confidence in working the resume.

The writer's tone is a result of word choice and is determined by the purpose and goal of a resume. The number of adjectives or adverbs used in conveying positive information will enhance the persuasiveness of any resume.

13.1.4 Presentation of Resumes

Together with letters of application, resumes play an indispensable role in the applicant's pursuit of desirable education, promising jobs, interesting hobbies, and colorful social activities. An effective resume often promises a better future in every aspect of personal development. A successful resume always follows some principles as listed below:

(1) Catching the Eyes of the Recipient

A piece of recruiting advertisement often brings hundreds of responses resembling each other in forms, contents, and styles. It is a boring job to read resumes that do not differentiate. A resume written in an individualized manner will infallibly catch the recipient's eyes and draw more attention from the recipient.

The individualization of a resume can be realized by adopting special manners of organizing the components that constitute the resume. For instance, the applicant can organize different types of information in relation to their importance. In addition, the applicant can use different fonts and different sizes of letters to draw the recipient's attention to what they care most.

(2) Catering to the Recipient's Requirements

A resume that is most successful in holding the recipient's attention is one that offers consistently what the recipient cares most. A resume that caters to the recipient's requirement will make them believe that what they are reading is not a waste of time.

(3) Showing Rather than Telling

Wrought to persuade the recipient into making a favorable response to the advantage of the applicant, a resume should try to avoid me-centered mentality.

Instead of using the personal pronoun "I" to tell personal information of various types in complete sentences, the resume writer can resort to noun phrases and verb phrases to show his qualifications and experience.

As phrases get right to the point, the resume writer is able to highlight what counts in his resume, which will in turn enable the reader to find out the attractive qualities of the resume writer.

(4) Using Informative Language

The language of resumes should be informative and factual, instead of being emphatic. The purpose of a resume is to convince the reader by facts rather than by cordial and persuasive language.

(5) Being Concise

Being written in phrases rather than complete sentences, the language of resumes should be concise and simple. It will enable the intended reader of them to catch the selling points of the resume writer within seconds.

13.1.5 Effective Resume Checklist

The following is a list of points to check when you write a resume.
- Is your objective clear?
- Have you included all the information that qualifies you for the objective?
- Have you included in your resume references which will make your personal data more reliable?
- Have you made your resume persuasive enough?
- Have you included in your resume information about your hobbies or interests that will arouse resonance in the intended reader of your resume?
- Have you adopted some highlighting techniques to ensure the accessibility of your resume?
- Have you used correct tone?
- Have you checked spelling, grammar and punctuation?

13.1.6 Sample Resumes

Sample 13.1 (1): A Resume Written to Apply for a Grant

Resume

Amy Gustavo Tan

May 26, 2007

City of Lancaster
120 N. Duke Street
P. O. Box 1599
Lancaster, PA - 17608 - 1599
(717) 291 - 4711

Experience

2004 - 2007	Advanced Accountant of Lancaster Retailing Center
2002 - 2004	General Accountant, Clean Cling Cosmetic Co., Ltd.
1998 - 2004	Executive Accountant, Special Metal Export Co., Ltd.
1994 - 1998	Assistant Accountant, A & B Interior Decorating Co., Ltd.

Education

1992 - 1994	Doing postgraduate work in Applied Accounting at Willington College
1988 - 1992	Wisconsin University, majored in Accounting

Qualifications
Proficient in accounting software
Skillful in budget control and taking sole responsibility
Licensed Accountant
Personal Data
Age: 35   Marital Status: Single
Hobby: collecting stamps, sports and reading
References
Mr. Leaning White,
Director of Data Processing, Big Brother Co., Ltd. Lancaster, PA 17608-1568
Telephone: (579) 456-9566

This resume is written in an intensive format.

Sample 13.1 (2): A Resume Applying for the Position of Translator or Interpreter

Oliver Steinbeck
123 Youth Road, New District, Suzhou 215004
Telephone: 0512-67220059
E-mail: oliversteinbeck@suda.edu.cn

Job Objective:

  Translator or interpreter

Qualifications

  Fluent in written and spoken English

  Fluent in written and spoken French

  Excellent at intercultural communications

  Competent in note taking and shorthand

Experience

  Co-translator of Prodigal Son (by William Arched, The Paradise Express), 2006

  Interpreter at the 100th China Import and Export Fair, Guangzhou, 2006

  Interpreter during the 28th Session of the World Culture and Heritage Committee, Suzhou, 2004

  Interpreter at the APEC Summit, 2004 in Shanghai

Education

* 2005.9-2007.6

  Soochow University, Suzhou

  Jiangsu, China

  Master Degree in Translation and Interpretation

* 2002.9-2005.7

  Shanghai International Studies University

Shanghai, China

B. A. in Translation and Interpretation

Certificates

* Advanced Interpretation, Shanghai
* Test for English Majors, Band 8
* Test for English Majors, Band 4

Reference

Available upon request

This is a resume written in the chronological order.

Sample 13.1 (3): A Resume Applying for the Position of Manager Assistant

Toad Eagleton

Room 203, Tehama Hall, California State University

400 West First Street, Chico, CA 95929-0145

Telephone: (530) 898-4015   E-mail: moiterry@hotmail.com

Job Intention

Manager Assistant which will lead to human resources management opportunities in a joint adventure or international operation

Summary of Qualifications

Expert at interpersonal communication; proficient at computer application; fluent in spoken and written English; two-year (2005-2007) working experience as manager assistant in Rocket Hi-Tech, Co., Ltd.

Management-oriented Education

Degree: Bachelor of Science, School of Business, California University, conferred in July 2005

Major: Business Management and Human Resources

Related Courses: International Management, Intercultural Communication, Computer Software Applications

Honor: Best Student of the Year, 2004

References

Professor Smith, California State University, (530) 898-4018

Professor Castro, California State University, (530) 898-4034

Bill Cliff, Manager, Rocket Hi-Tech, Co., Ltd. (530) 898-5037

This is a functional resume.

13.2 LETTERS OF APPLICATION

Letters of application, one of the most commonly used practical writing, address a specific person with a recognizable purpose of being admitted to an organization, or of being granted with some privileges. They are sent more often than not in response to advertisements by some organizations for the recruitment of new members or for the candidates of some offerings. Unlike a friendly letter which aims primarily to enhance friendship or to exalt familial ties, an application letter sets as its purpose to persuade the recipient to make a favorable offer in writing back.

Letters of application are widely used in job hunting, choosing a university to study at, applying for a grant, requesting for a membership at a club, etc.

To facilitate a successful outcome, letters of application should provide the necessary information that qualifies the applicant for the advertised membership or offerings. An applicant's degree, experience and other personal data are of paramount importance to the realization of the applicant's wishes.

Letters of application are often used together with resumes, which provide more detailed information about the applicant. They can also be used alone as unattached files, with resumes sent later upon further request made by the recipient.

There are many ways to send letters of application. Based on the different requirements set by different organizations, applications can be variously made in person, on line, via e-mail, or by resorting to the conventional delivery services. An application letter can then be presented in the format of booklet, the format of electronic file with given forms downloadable from the websites of some organizations, or the format of mail.

Some application letters are presented in the form of cover letter that forms part of a complete booklet. They are sent together with resumes or application forms that provide adequate information to qualify the applicant for the positions or benefits in question. This kind of application letters are always presented in person by the applicant to the personnel manager on the job market or at the manager's office when interviewed. The sincerity of the attitude and the faithfulness of the information conveyed in letters of this kind can be verified within seconds.

Another form letters of application might take is the electronic files, especially when the application is made on the websites of some organizations. Submitted together with the application letters are application forms demanding specific information of the applicants visiting such websites.

Letters of application can also be made in the format of mail when no application in person or application on line is available. Sending and receiving letters of application via e-mail are increasingly more popular with widespread easy access to the Internet almost everywhere.

13.2.1 The Layout of Letters of Application

An application letter should include the following information:
- Who writes the application letter? How to reach her/him?
- Who is the application letter written to? How to get into touch with the receiver of

the application letter?
- What is the writing purpose of the application letter?
- What qualifications does the applicant have?
- Does the applicant have any reference?
- Is there anything else attached to the application letter?
- What is the applicant's expectation?
- When will the applicant be convenient for an interview if there is any?

In a word, a letter of application often consists of five parts, namely the heading, the inside address, the greeting, the body, the complimentary close and the signature line. The five parts of a letter of application can be organized in three styles, namely the block style, the modified block style, and the semi-block style, as exemplified in the following examples.

Format 1

This is an example in the block style.

Format 2

This is an example in the modified block style.

Format 3

This is an example in the semi-block style.

Whatever style a letter of application may take, a line is to be skipped after each part except the complimentary close where two lines are to be skipped.

The heading in an application letter contains the return address followed by a line of date, sometimes with another few lines of a phone number, a fax number, an e-mail address, or the like imbedded in between.

The inside address always include titles, names, and routing information obtained from recruiting advertisements. It is the address that an application letter is sent to.

The greeting in an application letter normally begins with the word "Dear" and often includes the person's last name, which always has a title such as Mr., Mrs., Dr., or a political title. In letters of application, the greeting usually ends with colon.

The body of an application letter comprises three parts, namely the introductory paragraph, the main body and the closing paragraph. The introductory paragraph generally specifies why the applicant is writing the letter, whereas the main body expatiates on the personal qualities that will convince the recipient of the applicant's competence for what is being applied for. The closing paragraph, on the other hand, expresses the applicant's expectation for an interview at a convenient time with the recipient, as well the applicant's appreciation for the attention paid by the recipient.

The complimentary close customarily begins with a capital letter and ends with a comma.

The signature line is made up of the applicant's first name and last name. It may also include a middle initial, but does not have to. By placing Miss, Mrs., Ms. or similar title in parentheses before their name, women can indicate how they wish to be addressed. Two lines are to be skipped after the complimentary close. The signature line should be typed out in printed form. In the space between the close and the signature line, the applicant can sign in blue or black ink their name directly above the first letter of the signature line, though in many cases the signature is often omitted.

In the modified block style, as well as in the semi-block style, the heading is usually indented to the middle of the page. While in the block style, it begins at the left margin. Both the inside address and the greeting begin at the left margin in all styles. The first line of a new paragraph is indented in the semi-block style. The block and modified block style have all lines of the body to the left margin. The complimentary close and the signature line begin at the same column with the heading. A line is to be skipped after each part except the complimentary close where two lines are to be skipped. Skip a line between paragraphs if possible.

13.2.2 The Planning of Letters of Application

Letters of application follow the formal business letter style. To achieve their writing purpose, they should follow a direct organization plan. The steps in organizing a direct-plan application letter are: preparing the heading part, specifying the recipient's address, pinning down the writing purpose, planning the order of supporting details that exemplify the applicant's qualifications, presenting the applicant's expectations and concluding the letter of application.

The heading part will enable the recipient to send a favorable response to the right address. Similarly, the recipient's address will guarantee the timely arrival of the application letter at the recipient's address. The writing purpose will assure the recipient that the application letter is worth reading, while the qualifications will stimulate a favorable response from the recipient. The applicant's expectation as well as the polite conclusion will enhance the sincerity of the applicant in writing such an application letter.

Written to persuade the recipient to make a favorable reply to the applicant's advantage, the application letter should include positive information presented in a persuasive approach. When planning it, the applicant should choose what the recipient may be most interested in.

The general plan for a persuasive message is as follows. The opening sentences secure the recipient's attention by echoing the recipient's benefit, i. e. the writing of the application letter also meets the recipient's need to locate a most suitable candidate for a job vacancy or membership he/she holds or offers. The body intensifies the recipient's determination in offering an opportunity to the applicant by detailing the applicant's qualifications. The ending makes a request for an interview, which will be satisfied if the recipient is adequately persuaded.

13.2.3 The Tone of Letters of Application

The tone of an application letter refers to the applicant's voice. In writing an application letter, the applicant should follow some tips listed below:

(1) Being Sincere

Sincerity must mark the basic tone of a letter of application. It will more often than not draw the recipient to the applicant's side.

(2) Using Polite and Persuasive Language

Politeness in making a request will add force to the applicant's charm. On the other hand, it will constitute a sense of humbleness in presenting personal qualifications, which would otherwise appear too aggressive.

Persuasiveness should be another keynote of letters of application. The successfulness of an application letter relies largely on how persuasive it can be.

(3) Being Objective in Presenting Personal Qualifications

Objectivity in presenting personal qualifications will leave a positive impression upon the recipient of the application letter. Exaggeration in presenting personal ability will always induce the recipient into skipping over the application letter, thus skipping an opportunity which would have been given to the applicant.

13.2.4 Presentation of Letters of Application

The application letter is one of the most important documents in one's life career or personal development. An effective application letter often means an opportunity for an interview, but a poorly written one usually spells continued disattachment from any organization. The difference is just a matter of how to handle several key points. Here are some tips to present an effective letter of application.

(1) Individualizing the Application Letter

A recruiting advertisement often results in hundreds or even thousands of responses, some of which inevitably resemble one another in contents, forms or styles. To cut down the boredom on the part of the reader, the applicant should strive to avoid the simple borrowing of the forms and styles adopted in sample letters listed in reference books. Instead, the applicant should try to present their individuality and their distinct qualities.

(2) Addressing a Specific Person

Advisably, the person the applicant writes to should be the individual responsible for the recruiting task of a given organization. Search for the recipient's name in the recruiting advertisements, the organization's publications found at Placement Service, libraries or the websites of that organization. The correctness exhibited in the inside address of the recipient, as well as the addressing part, will demonstrate the applicant's sincerity and familiarity with the organization, which draws unconsciously the reader to the applicant's side.

(3) Catching the Recipient's Attention

An application letter should catch the recipient's attention, stimulate interest, and be appropriate for the membership being applied for. The applicant may, for example, begin the introductory paragraph either by referring to the advertisement that has prompted the application, or by discussing the organization that has put the advertisement. The knowledge of this kind will immediately inform the recipient of the effectiveness of the advertisement, and establish at the same time a touch of familiarity that spurs the recipient to read on for the benefit of the applicant.

To retain the recipient's attention, the applicant should assure the recipient that his goal of writing the application letter matches perfectly with their purpose of reading the application letter, and that they are not wasting their time reading the application letter. Therefore, it is crucial that the applicant make clear his goal in the introductory paragraph.

(4) Highlighting the Applicant's Qualifications

What encourages the recipient of an application letter to offer the applicant an opportunity is the applicant's qualifications, which they believe satisfy their requirements. So in an application letter, the applicant should list the merits that qualify him for what he is applying for.

The qualifications may include the applicant's educational background, work experience, personalities and strong suits. The recipient can refer to the resume for detailed information and letters of recommendation for the liability of the qualifications.

(5) Making Courteous Request

An application letter can conclude with a polite request for an interview to show the applicant's seriousness and eagerness in writing it. To relieve the recipient of the possible inconvenience in making a reply, the applicant should offer the means by which they can be reached. Be specific about the times and places that are convenient for an interview.

In the meantime, the applicant should also express his gratitude for the recipient's time and effort in reading the application letter.

Apart from following the tips expounded upon above, letters of application should not take too long to read. It should be short and simple.

13.2.5 Effective Application Letter Checklist

The following is a list of points to check when you write an application letter.
- Have you addressed your letter to the right person?
- Have you included in your letter your returning address?
- Have you made clear your writing purpose?
- Have you clarified your qualifications?
- Is your writing style consistent in format?
- Have you made a sincere request for a favorable reply?
- Have you achieved correct tone in your letter of application?
- Have you offered a time convenient for an interview?
- Is your application letter persuasive enough?
- Have you extended your appreciation for the recipient's time and effort in reading your letter?

13.2.6 Sample Letters of Application

Sample 13.2 (1): An Application Letter Answering a Job Advertisement

The following is an application letter written in modified block style in response to a piece of advertisement in newspapers for a position available to college graduates.

```
                                        Terry Moi
                                        Room 203, Tehama Hall
                                        College of Economics and Administration
                                        California State University, Chico
                                        400 West First Street
                                        Chico, CA 95929-0145
                                        Phone (530) 898-4015
                                        moiterry@hotmail.com
                                        May 27, 2019

Mr. Fidel Castro, Personnel Manager
Rose Merry Stock Exchange
Crystal Hall, 514
318 Eagle Street
Sacramento, CA 95814
```

Dear Mr. Castro,

    Your advertisement in *New York Times* for several Assistant Accountants greatly encouraged college graduates like me. My education and experience will assure you that I am just one of the most qualified candidates.

    The four-year study at the College of Economics and Administration, California State University has provided me with the systematic knowledge concerning accounting. Three years' experience as part-time accountant for several small firms has prepared me to handle problems in field work adequately well. Furthermore, my certificate as a licensed CPA (junior) in California lawfully qualifies me to start a job of Assistant Accountant in a renowned company like the Rose Merry Stock Exchange.

    I am available for an interview at your convenience every afternoon throughout the week. Professor Jennifer Hewitt, as well as Mr. Steven Cliff, the senior Accountant at the State Exchange, will be ready to attest my qualification to your advantage.

    Your consideration will be highly appreciated.

                                            Sincerely yours,
                                            Terry Moi
                                            Terry Moi

Encl: resume and two letters of recommendation

Sample 13.2 (2): An Application Letter in Block Style Applying for Admission to a Graduate School

Rong Chen
Department of Biology
Hebei Medial University
P. V. Box 206
361 Zhongshan Road
Shijiazhuang 050017, China
Tel: (86) 0311-86265504
Fax: (86) 0311-86265507
E-mail: rongchen@hotmail.com
July 24, 2019

Professor Christine Aniston
Integrated Graduate Program
Northwestern University Medical School
Ward 12-361 Mailcode W150
303 East Chicago Avenue
Chicago, IL 60611-3008

Dear Professor Aniston,

The postgraduate program on life science under your supervision really interests me. After reading the prospectus posted at the webpage power by Northwestern University, I find that I am qualified to become an international student there. So I am writing to see the possibility of doing my postgraduate work under your instruction.

I am to graduate with honor from Hebei Medical University in July, 2021. Well above the requirements set for international students (which requires an average GPA of 3.5, a TOFEL score of 580, and average GRE scores of 550 verbal and 650 quantitative), I have an average GPA of 4.0, a TOEFL score of 635 and a total of GRE scores of 1540 (verbal 780, quantitative 760).

So far as my major is concerned, I have been especially successful as a student of life science. I am the only student in my class who has got A^+ in all courses concerning biology and chemistry in past four years. In addition, I have also been awarded several prizes for my excellent performance in many research projects conducted by students. I have even published two papers in the renowned *Journal of Life Science*.

In view of my past academic achievement, I think I will have no difficulty in my postgraduate studies. It will be a great honor to be able to work under your guidance.

Enclosed please find two letters of recommendation and my resume.

Thank you for your consideration.

Yours faithfully,

Rong Chen

Rong Chen

Sample 13.2 (3): An Application Letter Applying for the Membership at the Designers' Club

	Carol Lopez
	The Sonic Designing Co., Ltd.
	235 Rainbow Street
	Madison, Wisconsin, 53717
	Tel: 1-608-2444703
	July 4, 2021
	clcarollopez@sonicdesigning.com
John Q. Hammons	
The Designers' Club	
Room 209, Crown Plaza Hotel	
Madison-East Towne	
4402E. Washington Ave	
Madison, WI 53704	

Dear Mr. Hammons,

Your advertisement for new club members in *Madison Evening* yesterday greatly excited me. Being an interior decoration designer, I have always been interested in sharing my working experience with others and doing my share to beautify our living environment. Now the Designers' Club just offers me such an opportunity.

I think I am qualified in many ways. First, I am a licensed interior decoration designer and also a Ph. D holder in art designer. I have both profound knowledge and field experience in interior decoration. The highly acclaimed Municipal Hall is one of my successful works. Second, I have taken part in various activities helping design for public facilities for free. I was the winner of best citizen in our neighborhood last year. In addition, I am also a guest professor in the Department of Art, University of Wisconsin. Currently, I am co-coaching some postgraduates with Professor Helen Fisher.

Please send me the application forms for admission and other relevant information. Thank you for your attention.

Respectfully yours,

Carol Lopez

Sample 13.2 (4): An Application Letter Applying for Scholarship

Letters of application for scholarship or grant share the same format and styles with letters of applying for admittance.

Allen Cooper
School of Foreign Languages
University of North Dakota
Grand Forks, ND 58202
allencooper@ uta. eud. cn
June 5, 2021

Eric Fabula, President
Dept. of Psychology
University of Utah
Admissions Office
201 S 1460 E Rm. 250 S
Salt Lake City, UT 84112 - 9057

Dear Mr. Eric Fabula,

I am writing to you in the hope of obtaining the Samaria Scholarship to support my study and research work on language learning and behavioral psychology.

I am a postgraduate student of linguistics at University of Dakota. Currently I am studying the mechanism of language learning in relation to behavioral psychology. Both to facilitate my research work and to push further the research done in this field, it is important that I work for a period of time at University of Utah to take advantage of the excellent educational resources and experiment devices there.

 Please find in my resume and two letters of recommendation my qualifications.

Thank you for your time and consideration. Look forward to your reply.

Cordially yours,
Allen Cooper

13.3 NOTES

(1) Different Types of Letters

 Letter writing normally falls into two categories: one is the formal business letter writing, and the other is the informal friendly letter writing. Letters of application belong to the category of formal business letters.

(2) Three Styles of Business Letters

 a. the block style 平头式

 b. the modified block style 改良平头式

 c. the semi-block style 半平头式

 In Format 1, Format 2 and Format 3, each picture represents a single page that carries a business letter on it. In each picture, the first three short lines (whether it is indented in the middle of the page or next to the left margin) near the top stands for the heading. The next three short lines next to the left margin stands for the inside address, beneath which the single line carries the greeting. The following two groups of lines indicate the body of an application letter. The last two short lines near the bottom refer to the complimentary close and the signature respectively.

(3) Different Ways of Application

 a. application made in person 现场申请/应聘

 b. application made on line 网站申请/应聘

 c. application made via mail 邮件申请/应聘

 d. application made via e-mail 电子邮件申请/应聘

(4) Different Formats of Letters of Application

 a. application letter in the format of cover letter 与简历、推荐信装订在一起成册且作为封面或内封面的申请函,往往当面递交

 b. application letter in the format of mail 信函式申请函

 c. application letter in the format of electronic files 通过招聘单位网站电子表格或程序递交的申请函

 d. application letter in the format of e-mail 电子邮件式申请函

(5) Enclosure/Encl/Enc: Resume / Letter of Recommendation 附:简历/推荐信

(6) Different Complimentary Close
   a. Sincerely yours
   b. Respectfully yours
   c. Cordially yours
   d. Yours faithfully
   e. Yours sincerely

(7) Classification of Resumes

   Different classifications of resumes are based on different ways of information organization. Information organized in extensive resumes is similar to that in chronological resumes. Likewise, the organization of information in intensive resumes is almost the same as that in resumes written in the functional style. In a word, they are just different terms for the same resumes.

(8) Different Forms of Resumes

   Resumes are customarily written in the format of text paying special attention to different types of information on the same page. Occasionally, applicant can also draw a form to put different items of information into different grids. Resumes written in this format are much similar to application forms.

(9) Useful Expressions
   * expert at ...
   * proficient in ...
   * have a sound knowledge of ...
   * have experience in ...
   * skillful in interpersonal and intercultural communication
   * a good understanding and working knowledge of computers
   * three years of experience in personnel recruiting ...
   * field experience in ...
   * working as a ... part time
   * secretary to / assistant to ...
   * ready to travel ...
   * licensed Account registered at National Accounting Association
   * certificate for ...
   * Computer Proficiency Test
   * major in ... and minor in ...
   * M. A. to be conferred in June 2022
   * educational background in human resources ...
   * university education in ...
   * available upon further request
   * I am writing to you in the hope ...
   * I wish to apply for the position mentioned in your advertisement ...

* Your advertisement for ... greatly interested me.
* I take the liberty of writing to you to apply for ...
* I learned from that ... your company is to recruit some new members.
* So I am writing to see the possibility of ...
* My education and experience will assure you that I am just one of the most qualified candidates ...
* Enclosed please find ...
* Thank you for your time and consideration.
* Your attention will be highly appreciated.
* Enclosed is my resume and application form.
* It will be a great honor to be able to work in your company.
* Your prompt reply in this matter would be sincerely appreciated.
* I will be available for an interview at any time in your convenience.
* Professor Smith will be on my side to attest to my ...

13.4 COMMUNICATION LABORATORY

A. **Give a brief answer to the following questions.**
   (1) What are the functions of a resume?
   (2) How to write an effective resume?
   (3) What are the features of the language used in a resume?
   (4) What are the differences between resumes and letters of application?
   (5) What are the functions of letters of application?
   (6) What are the features of the language used in application letters?
   (7) How can an application letter be effectively made?
   (8) What are the differences between different styles of application letters?
   (9) In what ways can an application letter be sent?

B. **Case Study**
   (1) Write a resume in response to an advertisement recruiting entry-level technicians assembling cars.
   (2) Write a resume to the university where you want to pursue your first degree in art.
   (3) Analyze the following application letter and try to point out the problems in it.

Dear Sir or Madam,

 I am a successful learner of economic at State University of Pennsylvania. I am second in all subjects in my class.

 I have worked part-time as a sales representative for a couple of big business corporations. I have also been crazily involved in starting my own business in cooperation of my friends. Experience accumulated from these activities has given deep insight into the essence of successful business activities.

 Enclosed please find my resume and two recommendation letters.

Sincerely yours,
Andrew

(4) Write an application letter based on the following situations.

 ① Write an application letter in response to the following advertisement.

Advance Secretary Wanted

 M. A. holder, major in English, foreign trade or related field

 Registered at National Secretary Association

 Over 10 years' experience working as a secretary for joint ventures

 Overseas experience preferred

Doris Remedy, Personnel Manager

Terrain Hi-tech Co., Ltd.

345 Sussex St.

New York, New York 14355

Tel: 1 - 508 - 5444703

dorisremedy@ terrainhitech. com

May 18, 2021

 ② Apply for admission at Stanford University.

Unit 14 Certificates and Credentials

Certificates and credentials are quite formal writings and documents both in content and in format. They are issued officially by an authorized organization, committee, educational institution, etc.

The formal and official nature of certificates and credentials determines the formality of language and format used in those official documents.

Certificates and credentials should include:
- The classifications of the certificates or credentials issued, e. g. Certificate of Graduation, Certificate of Achievement;
- Detailed information about the person to whom the certificates or credentials are issued;
- An official stamp or seal where necessary;
- The signature of the head of an authorized organization, committee, educational institution;
- The time and date of the issue of the certificates or credentials.

14.1 THE LAYOUT OF CERTIFICATES AND CREDENTIALS

The Heading (the Nature of the Certificate)

This is to certify (I hereby certify) WHO, THE DATE OF BIRTH, WHAT, THE DURATION OF TIME, and THE PROPOSED ACHIEVEMENTS.

Official Stamp or Seal	The Name of Institution
Date	Signature

Unit 14　Certificates and Credentials

14.2　SAMPLE CERTIFICATES AND CREDENTIALS

Sample 14（1）

Certificate of Graduation　　　　　　No. 060812

PHOTO

　　I hereby certify that Chen Ping, male, aged 24, a student from Shanghai, who was admitted to the English Major of the School of Foreign Languages, in September 2017, has completed four years' courses and, having fulfilled all the requirements set by the syllabus, graduated from Jiangsu University of Science and Technology.

(STAMP)

Jiangsu University of Science and Technology

(Signature)

President

July 2, 2021

Sample 14（2）

The regents of the
UNIVERSITY OF MINNESOTA
on the recommendation of the faculty
have conferred upon
John D. Kennedy
the degree of
Master of Social Work

With all its privileges and obligations
given at Duluth, in the State of Minnesota,
this nineteenth day of August, nineteen hundred eighty-three.

(signature)	(signature)
SECRETATY, BORAD OF REGENTS	PRESIDENT
(signature)	(signature)
DAEN, GRADUATE SCHOOL	CHANCELLOR

Sample 14 (3)

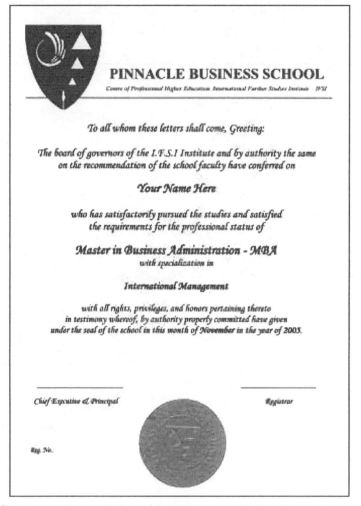

Sample 14 (4)

Certificate of Graduation

I hereby certify that Zhou Li, female, aged 24, was a student of the International Business Major of the School of Business and, having completed the four years' courses from September 2017 to July 2021 and fulfilled all the requirements set by the syllabus, graduated from Jiangsu University in July 2021.
 	
(STAMP)
 	
    (Signature)
    President
    Jiangsu University

Sample 14 (5)

> Wang Bin, a student of Grade 2019 from Jiangsu University, who took the Test of English Majors (Grade 4) organized and administered by the English Group of the Teaching Guiding Committee for College Foreign Language Majors under the Ministry of Education, has passed all the requirements and is hereby granted the Certificate of TEM-4.
>
> The Teaching Guiding Committee
for College Foreign Language Majors
(STAMP)
>
> Certificate Number: 200645788

Sample 14 (6)

> Wang Jun, a student of Grade 2019 from Jiangsu University of Science and Technology, who took the Test of English Majors (Grade 8) organized and administered by the English Group of the Teaching Guiding Committee for College Foreign Language Majors under the Ministry of Education, has passed all the requirements and is hereby granted the Certificate of TEM-8.
>
> The Teaching Guiding Committee
for College Foreign Language Majors
(STAMP)
>
> Certificate Number: 200610024

Sample 14 (7)

> **The Report Card of**
College English Test (CET-Band 4)
>
> Name: Zhang Yin
> University (College): Jiangsu University of Science and Technology
> School (Department): Computer Sciences
> Test Registry Number: 321311105100126
> ID Number: 321102840501404
> Time of Test: June 2019
>
> PHOTO
>
> Total Score: 558
>
> | Listening (20%) | Reading (40%) | Comprehensive (25%) | Writing (15%) |
> | --- | --- | --- | --- |
> | 131 | 197 | 162 | 68 |
>
> Report Card No: 051132131003448
>
> The Higher Education Department of
China's Ministry of Education
(STAMP)
Issued by: National Testing
Committee for College English Test
(Band 4 and Band 6)

Sample 14 (8)

The Report Card of
College English Test (CET-Band 6)

Name: Wang Dongming
University (College): Jiangsu University
School (Department): Electrical Engineering
Test Registry Number: 321311105100126
ID Number: 321102860403
Time of Test: June 2019

PHOTO

Total Score: 540

Listening (20%)	Reading (40%)	Comprehensive (25%)	Writing (15%)
130	186	162	62

Report Card No.: 051132131001174

The Higher Education Department of
China's Ministry of Education
(STAMP)

Issued by: National Testing Committee
for College English Test
(Band 4 and Band 6)

Sample 14 (9)

  Zhu Jun, a student from Shanghai University, having passed the yearly test of 2019 for non-computer sciences majors in the knowledge and aptitude of computer application, is hereby conferred this certificate.

  Test Grade and Language: Grade 1, Windows

Shanghai Education Bureau
(STAMP)

Date: December 2019
Certificate No.: 200665118709

Sample 14（10）

Certificate of Achievement

This is to certify that

Wang Tongming

has successfully completed the
International Business Institute Program
under the joint auspices of
Educational Services Exchange with China
Jiangsu University of Science and Technology

Educational Services Exchange with China（ESEC）（STAMP）
Jiangu University of Science and Technology（STAMP）

Sample 14（11）

Certificate

This is to certify that Ms. Zhang Hong
has passed the Business English Test
（Vantage Level）

　　　　　　　　　　　　　　　　　　Jiangsu Business English Test Center

Date of Issue: September 2019　　　　　　　　　　　　　　（STAMP）

Sample 14（12）

Certificate

This certificate is awarded to

　　　　　　　　　　　　　　　　　　　　　　　　　　Yang Fan

The First Prize Winner of the 11th English Speaking Contest jointly hosted by the Youth League Committee and School of Foreign Languages of Jiangsu University.

　　　　　　　　　　　　　　　Youth League Committee of Jingsu University

September 20, 2019　　　　　　　　　　　　　　　　　　（STAMP）

　　　　　　　　　　　School of Foreign Languages of Jiangsu University

　　　　　　　　　　　　　　　　　　　　　　　　　　（STAMP）

176　A Practical Coursebook for Business English Writing

Sample 14（13）

Certificate of Honor

This is to certify that Wang Lingling has been awarded the title of

Model Student

in the Social Work of College Students conducted in 2019 Summer Vacation organized and sponsored by Jiangsu University of Science and Technology.

September 2019　　　　　　　　　　　　　　　　　　　　　Youth League Committee

　　　　　　　　　　　　　　　　　　　　　Jiangsu University of Science and Technology

---

Sample 14（14）

High School Diploma

　I hereby certify that Zhang Yan, female, born on March 14, 1986, was a student from Nanjing, has studied in the senior section for three years (September 2003 – July 2006) and has completed all the courses and met all the requirements set by the high school syllabus, and graduated from the school.

(STAMP)

　　　　　　　　　　　　　　　　　　　　　　　　　　　　　　(Signature)
　　　　　　　　　　　　　　　　　　　　　　　　　　　　　　Principal
　　　　　　　　　　　　　　　　　　　　　　　　　　　Nanjing Yucai High School

14.3　NOTES

(1) certificate of academic degrees　学位证书
(2) certificate of graduation　毕业证书
(3) president　（大学）校长
(4) diploma　文凭
(5) certificate of honor　荣誉证书
(6) certificate of achievement (completion)　结业证书
(7) certificate of completion/incompletion/attendance/study　肄业证书
(8) certificate of commendation　奖状
(9) letter of appointment　聘任书
(10) This is to certify …　兹证明……
(11) Regulations Concerning Academic Degrees in the People's Republic of China
　　《中华人民共和国学位条例》

（12）college/institute of education　教育学院

（13）normal specialized postsecondary college　师范专科学校

（14）normal/teachers' university　师范大学

（15）radio and television university　广播电视大学

（16）self-study examination　自学考试

（17）vocational university　职业大学

（18）training program　培训课程（计划）

（19）a three-year program in colleges　专科

（20）a four-year program in universities/colleges　本科

14.4　COMMUNICATION LABORATORY

Translate the following certificates and credentials into English and pay close attention to the format.

（1）　　　　　　　　　　中级英语口语培训班结业证书

　　王红,女,现年 25 岁,在××大学外国语学院外语培训中心完成为期 4 个月的中级英语口语培训,成绩合格,准予结业,特此证明。

××大学外国语学院
外语培训中心
（公章）
二〇一九年一月

（2）　　　　　　　　　　毕业证书

　　学生　张军,性别　男,江苏　省　南京　市人,一九八四年五月十五日生,二〇〇二年九月至二〇〇六年七月　在本校外国语学院　英语专业　肆年制本科就读,修业期满,成绩合格,准予毕业。

学校印章

××大学
校长
（签名）

（3）　　　　　　　　　　荣誉证书

　　王强　老师讲授的《商务英语函电》课程荣获 2018/2019 学年校"优秀教学质量奖"。特发此证

××科技大学
（公章）
二〇一九年十月

Unit 15 Public Signs

Public signs are usually public marks with tag definitions attached to them or description integrated with the marks as a whole. Generally speaking, a public sign consists of two parts: a mark or figure that symbolizes certain actions or things and a description about what is embodied within the mark or figure. However, not every public sign contains a picture or figure to imitate the action to be taken by people or the things people want to have knowledge of. The term "public sign" can be used narrowly to refer to the description that informs people of what shall be done or what they want to learn about.

Public signs are always about what to do, what shall not be done, where to go, and how to do, as well as what people can get or what people are entitled to. In a sense, pubic signs are simplified but more vivid version of notices. They are seen almost everywhere in public places helping people with their life.

According to their different functions, public signs can be classified roughly into four groups. They are public signs guiding people about what to do, when to come or leave, where to go, how to do, and why to do, public signs suggesting proper and civilized behavior, public signs representing particular places, and public signs telling people about what they are entitled to, all of which cover almost all aspects of public life. The first two types of public signs are usually instructions leading to specific actions on the part of the viewers. The last two types of public signs always provide various types of information for the convenience or to the advantage of the viewers, who will either accept or just turn down the convenience or advantage offered. The classification of public signs of this kind is not made to the exclusion of others. Different groups of public signs may overlap.

As a code of public behavior, public signs in a given country are usually written to the advantage of native people in the official language of that country. However, public signs written in English are playing a more and more important role in China today as thousands of foreigners rush into China everyday. Wrongly wrought public signs will bring about not only great inconvenience for foreigners living or traveling in China, but even great losses in business domains to businessmen of all kinds. Therefore, it is important to get a thorough knowledge about public signs before starting to create effective and powerful public signs.

15.1 THE LAYOUT OF PUBLIC SIGNS

Public signs giving instructions normally contain two parts. Because they exist to guide people about their behaviors in public spheres, public signs usually contain an imperative action and an object which is the target of the action.

The imperative action always refers to the action expected of people in public. The carrying out of such an action suggests the norms governing people's behavior in public spheres. The imperative action can be realized by using verbs used in imperative forms. For example, "Push the door outward". It can also be realized by using emphatic negative word "no" in capital forms at the cost of the imperative verbs. In this case, a simple but most frequently seen example is "No Smoking". In addition, the verb "be" in imperative forms can used together with some adjectives that suggest some aspects of life for the same effect. For example, "Be Kind to the Grasses". To indicate politeness in delivering instructions, the word "please" is often used as in "Please do not park here".

On the other hand, the object in a public sign usually indicates a specific domain of public life. It is the reality that people want to keep or it is the specific phenomenon people want to get rid of. A violation of it always suggests an improper deed and often means some kind of punishment, while adherence to it often indicates some desirable personal traits or some benefits. For example, the "grass" in "Please keep off the grass" suggests part of the beautiful environment, natural and artificial alike. Sometimes, the punishment suggested by a public sign can be used together with the sign to demonstrate directly what consequence a person's inappropriate action in public might bring about, for instance "Private use only. Unauthorized parking will be fined".

There are also many signs which contain only the object part sometimes to be modified by specific nouns or adjectives to convey the actions required of people in public. For instance, the public sign "Pay Toilet". It means that people have to pay for the use of it.

Sometimes, public signs giving instructions will be introduced by several words that delineate the situations in which specific deeds on the part of the sign reader are expected. For example, "Hot! Avoid Contact", and "Out of use, please use the other doors".

Public signs providing information for the convenience or to the advantage of the viewers of those signs may also contain two parts, namely the part that indicates certain convenience or advantage, and the part that describes the kind of convenience or advantage available to the viewers, though the latter of which is not always indispensable. For example, "Fresh Produce". The word "produce" represents all kinds of the farming goods which are indispensable to people's life and the word "fresh" enhances further the benefits people might get.

Whatever parts or however many parts a public sign may contain, it generally

includes the following information:
- What is the public sign about?
- To whom is the public sign addressed?
- What function(s) will the public sign enact?
- What benefit will the public sign bring about for the viewer of it?
- What obligation is required of the viewer of the public sign?
- What action is expected of the viewer of the public sign?

The information listed above should be positioned as shown in the following examples.

Format 1

> NO STOPPING!

This is a public sign addressed to car owners or other vehicle owners. It is required of them not to park their cars or other vehicles at the place where this public sign is posted. This sign is publicized either to guarantee the issuer's privacy or to maintain the order in public spheres. The message is conveyed in a noun preceded by the emphatic negative "NO".

Format 2

> DO NOT BREAK SEALS. NO FUSES INSIDE.

This is a public sign issued to warn anybody who intends to open the electric device against any possible electrical shock. The message is conveyed in an imperative sentence together with a noun phrase preceded by the emphatic negative "NO".

Format 3

> Ticket & Travel Centre

This public sign is addressed to travelers in want of tickets or any other kind of travel service. It is conveyed in phrases only.

Format 4

This is a public sign encouraging people to keep public sanitation. The message is conveyed with a symbol describing a dog owner cleaning the dog's dejectas.

Public signs often appear in a bulletin board attached to walls, posts or some other things in public places. They also appear as posters attached to things aforementioned. Owing both to the little space in which they are printed and to the fact that they are created to stimulate prompt action or to inform of instant knowledge within seconds, public signs often take just a few lines that are easy to discern and quick to understand. To make the message more effective, they often appear together with instructive figures or pictures, and take the form of captions.

As far as the ways they are conveyed, public signs customarily fall into two types, namely public signs written in phrases, and public signs written in complete sentences. The following are two more examples that exemplify the two forms of public signs respectively: "Mercury Free" and "For security reasons, please keep your bags and personal belongings with you all the time. Thank you for your vigilance".

15.2 THE PLANNING OF PUBLIC SIGNS

Like notices posted in public places, most public signs follow a direct organization plan. The steps in organizing a direct-plan public signs are: identifying the public sphere where the public sign is to be posted, specifying the group of people to be governed by the public sign, formulating the response required of the target group of people or the benefit promised for those people, and finally conveying the message with the help of suitable figures or symbols if necessary.

Occasionally, some public signs regulating improper public behaviors may involve the taboos of a given culture. The direct organization approach may then constitute a part of indecent public life and may therefore prove unacceptable. In this case, an indirect organization plan may be adopted.

15.3 THE TONE OF PUBLIC SIGNS

When you are creating a public sign, you are writing either to enact suitable behavior in public or to inform the public of their obligations or privileges. Therefore, the tone of public signs should be both persuasive and instructive.

The message in a public sign should be conveyed in such a manner that it would be helpful in the building of public comity. For this reason, it should also be conveyed in a polite tone. It can be realized by the frequent use of the courteous words like "please" and "thank you".

15.4 PRESENTATION OF PUBLIC SIGNS

Since public signs are designed to regulate people's behavior, effective public signs are those which are most successful in guiding people about their life in public areas. Here are some tips about how to present the message of public signs.

(1) Being Succinct in Giving Instructions

Since most public signs are instructions regulating people's behavior in public, they should be simple to understand and easy to be carried out. If a public sign were written in a long passage composed of complicated sentences, it is almost impossible for people to understand what it means and carry out what is expected of them the moment they pass it. Therefore, most public signs are always written only in a few lines. In some cases, some public signs are just conveyed in several words or even the initials of some words. A case in point is the commonly seen public sign of "WC" in China, though it is criticized by some as an improper public sign.

(2) Choosing Correct Words

Apart from using courteous words, public signs should also be explicit and accurate in meaning. A failure of this often leads to confusions. For example, the public sign of "Racist Park" in Beijing. Does it refer to a park where racism prevails? Won't it be more acceptable if it is put into "Park of Ethnic Minorities"? More examples with misleading meanings would be like this: "Please only put toilet tissue down the toilet", "Business Suspended", "No dogs bikes skates skateboarding", "Rope Way Station" and so on.

(3) Using Supplementary Figures or Pictures

Public signs used together with figures or pictures are always easier to understand than those with no supplementary figures or pictures. It is largely because language is abstract whereas pictures or figures are concrete. For example, a simple public sign that "Thank you for clearing up" can be open to different interpretations if it is not accompanied with a picture in which the owner is clearing away the ordure produced by his dog. However, a badly designed figure is as misleading as bad public signs.

(4) Using Standardized Language

A public sign written in slang or idiom is always unacceptable to the wide public. As its name suggests, a public sign should use standardized language to convey what it attempts to express.

(5) Highlighting the Message

Since public signs are posted in public places to inform the public of given subjects, they should be conveyed in such a manner that it would be easy to catch people's eyes. Therefore, words spelled in capital form or bold form can be adopted. Similarly, special fonts and color can also be used to attract the public.

15.5 EFFECTIVE PUBLIC SIGN CHECKLIST

The following is a list of points to check when you create a public sign.
- Have you used correct format?

- Have you adopted correct tone in conveying the message?
- Have you included all the relevant information?
- Have you made your purpose clear?
- Is your writing style concise?
- Have you made your public signs appealing to the eye?

15.6 SAMPLE PUBLIC SIGNS

Sample 15 (1): Public Signs about Proper Behavior

Sample 15 (2): Public Signs Guiding People Where to Go

Sample 15 (3): Public Signs Telling People of Their Rights

Sample 15 (4): Public Signs Telling People What to Do

Sample 15（5）：Public Signs Telling People What Not to Do

Sample 15（6）：Public Signs Indicating Special Places

15.7 NOTES

（1）Pay Toilet 收费厕所
An improper alternative widely used to "Pay Toilet" is "Colleting Free Toilet".

（2）Please only put toilet tissue down the toilet. 仅将厕纸冲入厕所。
This sign is really misleading and it will make people wonder if it is all right to use the toilet device there at all.

（3）Business Suspended 暂停营业
This sign may make people wonder that the service is stopped suddenly in the middle.

（4）No dogs bikes skates skateboarding. 人行道上自行车禁行。
It is originally used to stop the use of bicycles, does not rule out of the possibility of riding bicycle on the pavements.

（5）Rope Way Station 缆车乘客中心
This sign refers to nothing but the station where people wait for cable cars.

（6）Please do not park here. 此处禁止停车。

（7）Please keep off the grass. 请爱护花草/请勿践踏草坪！

（8）Park of Ethnic Minorities 少数民族公园

（9）Private use only. Unauthorized parking will be fined. 严禁外来车辆停车，违者罚款。

（10）Fresh Produce 新鲜农产品

（11）Be kind to grass. 爱护花草。

（12）Thank you for cleaning up. 请随手清除宠物粪便,谢谢合作。

（13）Thank you for keeping your voices down. 请勿大声喧哗。

（14）Dogs must be on leash at all times. 宠物狗须一直用狗链拴着。

（15）Bike Route   自行车道

（16）Bus Parking Ahead   前方停车场

（17）Authorized Vehicles Only   未经许可，车辆不准停放

（18）Authorized Personnel Only   未经许可，不得入内/闲人莫入

（19）Staff Only   仅对员工开放

（20）Ring bell for service.   如需服务，请按铃。

（21）Push for emergency.   如有紧急情况，请按此键钮。

（22）Taking Board Pass   刷卡通过

（23）Wet Paint   油漆未干，请勿触摸

（24）Warning! Security Dog!   小心，有看门狗！

（25）This is a smoke free station.   此车站严禁吸烟。

15.8 COMMUNICATION LABORATORY

A. **Give a brief answer to the following questions.**

（1）What are public signs?

（2）What are the functions of public signs?

（3）What are the differences between public signs and notices?

B. **Case Study**

（1）Improve the public signs listed below.

   a. Please only put toilet tissue down the toilet.

   b. Business Suspended

   c. No dogs bikes skates skateboarding.

   d. Rope Way Station

（2）Write some public signs based on the following situations. Use figures or pictures to clarify the public signs when necessary.

   a. It is dangerous for passengers to get on the train with things that are easy to catch fire.

   b. We have some guests here and please don't make any noise.

   c. Warn people that it is a route leading to nowhere.

   d. Warn drivers to slow down because there is a kindergarten ahead.

（3）Try to find out some public signs that need improvement in China.

Unit 16　Questionnaires

Questionnaires are an inexpensive way to gather data from a potentially large number of respondents. Often they are the only feasible way to reach a number of reviewers large enough to allow statistical analysis of the results. A well-designed questionnaire that is used effectively can gather information on both the overall performance of the test system as well as information on specific components of the system. If the questionnaire includes demographic questions on the participants, they can be used to correlate performance and satisfaction with the test system among different groups of users.

It is important to remember that a questionnaire should be viewed as a multi-stage process beginning with definition of the aspects to be examined and ending with interpretation of the results. Every step needs to be designed carefully because the final results are only as good as the weakest link in the questionnaire process. Although questionnaires may be cheap to administer compared to other data collection methods, they are every bit as expensive in terms of design time and interpretation.

16.1　THE STEPS REQUIRED TO DESIGN AND ADMINISTER A QUESTIONNAIRE

- Defining the Objectives of the Survey
- Determining the Sampling Group
- Writing the Questionnaire
- Administering the Questionnaire
- Interpreting of the Results

16.2　POINTS CONSIDERED WHEN WRITING AND INTERPRETING QUESTIONNAIRES

Clarity. This is probably the area that causes the greatest source of mistakes in questionnaires. Questions must be clear, succinct, and unambiguous. The goal is to eliminate the chance that the question will mean different things to different people. If the designers fail to do this, then essentially participants will be answering different questions.

To this end, it is best to phrase your questions empirically if possible and to avoid the use of necessary adjectives. For example, if asking a question about frequency, rather than supplying choices that are open to interpretation such as:

(1) Very Often

(2) Often

(3) Sometimes

(4) Rarely

(5) Never

It is better to quantify the choices, such as:

(1) Every Day or More

(2) 2-6 Times a Week

(3) About Once a Week

(4) About Once a Month

(5) Never

Leading Questions. A leading question is one that forces or implies a certain type of answer. It is easy to make this mistake not in the question, but in the choice of answers. A closed format question must supply answers that not only cover the whole range of responses, but that are also equally distributed throughout the range. All answers should be equally likely. An obvious, nearly comical, example would be a question that supplies these answer choices:

(1) Superb

(2) Excellent

(3) Great

(4) Good

(5) Fair

(6) Not So Great

A less blatant example would be a Yes/No question that asked:

> Is this the best CAD interface you have ever used?

In this case, even if the participant loved the interface, but had a favorite that was preferred, she would be forced to answer No. Clearly, the negative response covers too wide a range of opinions. A better way would be to ask the same question but supply the following choices:

(1) Totally Agree

(2) Partially Agree

(3) Neither Agree or Disagree

(4) Partially Disagree

(5) Totally Disagree

This example is also poor in the way it asks the question. Its choice of words makes it a leading question and a good example for the next section on phrasing.

Phrasing. Most adjectives, verbs, and nouns in English have either positive or negative connotations. Two words may have equivalent meaning, yet one may be a compliment and the other an insult. Consider the two words "child-like" and "childish", which have virtually identical meaning. Child-like is an affectionate term that can be applied to both men and women, and young and old, yet no one wishes to be thought of as childish.

A more subtle, but no less troublesome, example can be made with verbs that have neither strong negative nor positive overtones. Consider the following two questions:

> —Do you agree with the Governor's plan to oppose increased development of wetlands?
> —Do you agree with the Governor's plan to support curtailed development of wetlands?

They both ask the same thing, but will possibly produce different data. One asks in a positive way, and the other in a negative. It is impossible to predict how the outcomes will vary, so one method to counter this is to be aware of different ways to word questions and provide a mix in your questionnaire. If the participant pool is very large, several versions may be prepared and distributed to cancel out these effects.

Embarrassing Questions. Embarrassing questions dealing with personal or private matters should be avoided. Your data are only as good as the trust and care that your respondents give you. If you make them feel uncomfortable, you will lose their trust. Do not ask embarrassing questions.

Prestige Bias. Prestige bias is the tendency for respondents to answer in a way that makes them feel better. People may not lie directly, but may try to put a better light on themselves. For example, it is not uncommon for people to respond to a political opinion poll by saying they support Samaritan social programs, such as food stamps, but then go on to vote for candidates who oppose those very programs. Data from other questions, such as those that ask how long it takes to learn an interface, must be viewed with a little skepticism. People tend to say they are faster learners than they are.

There is little that can be done to prevent prestige bias. Sometimes there just is no way to phrase a question so that all the answers are noble. The best means to deal with prestige bias is to make the questionnaire as private as possible. Telephone interviews are better than person-to-person interviews, and written questionnaires mailed to participants are even better still. The farther away the critical eye of the researcher is, the more honest the answers.

16.3 SAMPLE QUESTIONNAIRES

Sample 16（1）

Product Quality Questionnaire

1. Have you ever purchased a cell phone in the past two years?
   ☐ Yes   ☐ No   ☐ Cannot remember
2. Which brand did you choose?
   ☐ Nokia
   ☐ Samsung
   ☐ A domestic brand（please specify）
3. Are you satisfied with the cell phone?
   ☐ Yes   ☐ No   ☐ Hard to say
4. Are you satisfied with the price?
   ☐ Yes   ☐ No   ☐ Not sure
5. Is the product durable or long lasting?
   ☐ Yes
   ☐ No
   ☐ Hard to say as I have just bought it
6. Has the cell phone ever been repaired?
   ☐ Yes   ☐ No
7. Is deluxe packing necessary?
   ☐ Yes   ☐ No   ☐ No idea
8. Is after-sale service good enough?
   ☐ Yes   ☐ No
9. Do you have any complaints about the cell phone?
   ☐ Yes（please specify） ☐ No
10. Do you have any suggestions?
    ☐ Yes（please specify） ☐ So far no
11. Are you going to buy anything from the same producer?
    ☐ Yes   ☐ No   ☐ Not sure
12. Please indicate your gender, age and occupation.
    _____

Sample 16（2）

Service Quality Questionnaire

1. Have you ever dined in or purchased any fast food from KFC in the past week?
   ☐ Yes   ☐ No   ☐ Cannot remember
2. How often do you eat KFC fast food?
   ☐ Once a week   ☐ Once every other week
   ☐ Once a month   ☐ Others

3. When you'd like to eat KFC fast food, do you usually: (Tick only one)
   ☐ Have it delivered to your house?
   ☐ Have it delivered to your place of work?
   ☐ Pick it up yourself?
   ☐ Just dine at a KFC outlet?
4. How do you like the KFC fast food taste? (Tick only one)
   ☐ Excellent   ☐ Good   ☐ Fair   ☐ Poor
5. How do you think you are served?
   ☐ Well enough   ☐ Satisfactorily   ☐ Poorly
6. Do all the waiters and waitresses wear a pleasant smile when they serve you?
   ☐ Yes   ☐ No   ☐ No idea
7. How do you rate the response to your request for any kind of in-restaurant service?
   ☐ Very prompt   ☐ Prompt   ☐ Delayed   ☐ Very slow
8. Do you have any complaints?
   ☐ Yes (please specify)   ☐ No
9. Do you have any suggestions?
   ☐ Yes (please specify)   ☐ No
10. Please indicate your gender, age and occupation.
    _____

Sample 16 (3)

Questionnaire on Campus Activities

1. Does your university, college or department often organize extra-curricular activities?
   ☐ Yes   ☐ No   ☐ Don't know
2. Do you think your university, college or department should organize more campus activities?
   ☐ Yes   ☐ No   ☐ Hard to say
3. Do you think campus activities can enrich your campus life?
   ☐ Yes   ☐ No   ☐ Not sure
4. Do you think too much devotion to campus activities might spoil your studies?
   ☐ Yes   ☐ No   ☐ Hard to say
5. Are you an active participant of campus activities?
   ☐ Yes
   ☐ No
   ☐ I only participate in what I am interested in
6. Do you think those activities are well-organized?
   ☐ Yes   ☐ No   ☐ Some are and some aren't
7. Do you agree that campus activities are nothing but a waste of time?
   ☐ Yes (please justify your argument)   ☐ No   ☐ Not sure
8. Do you think well-organized campus activities can help us foster our comprehensive abilities?
   ☐ Yes   ☐ No   ☐ Hard to say

9. Why do you participate in campus activities?
   ☐ Just for fun
   ☐ To kill time
   ☐ To enrich my campus life
   ☐ To further improve my communicative abilities
10. Have you got any suggestions about campus activities?
    ☐ Yes (please specify)   ☐ No
11. Please indicate your major, gender and age.
    _____

Sample 16 (4)

Questionnaire on Classroom Teaching

1. Do you think your teachers are fully committed to classroom teaching?
   ☐ Yes   ☐ No   ☐ Some teachers are and some are not
2. Do you think your teachers attach importance to their teaching approaches?
   ☐ Yes   ☐ No   ☐ Don't know
3. Do you agree that classroom teaching should be student-centered?
   ☐ Yes   ☐ No   ☐ Not sure
4. Some students say classroom teaching is totally teachers' business, do you agree?
   ☐ Yes   ☐ No   ☐ Hard to say
5. Do you think your teachers have done a good job so far in cultivation of your interest in their lectures?
   ☐ Yes   ☐ No   ☐ No idea
6. Do you think it is necessary for teachers to use multi-media resources to facilitate their teaching?
   ☐ Yes   ☐ No   ☐ Hard to say
7. What do you think of bilingual teaching adopted by some teachers?
   ☐ Very good   ☐ Good   ☐ Not so good
8. What do you think is the most important qualification for a teacher? (Tick only one)
   ☐ Responsibility   ☐ Knowledgeableness   ☐ Easy to communicate with
9. Generally speaking, are you satisfied with the classroom teaching on your teachers' part?
   ☐ Yes   ☐ No   ☐ No comment
10. Please indicate your major, gender and age.
    _____

Sample 16 (5)

Questionnaire on College Students' Monthly Expenditures

1. Do you come from urban areas or rural areas?
   ☐ Urban areas ☐ Rural areas
2. Which province or city do you come from? (Please specify)
   _____
3. Are both of your parents employed?
   ☐ Yes ☐ No (If no, please specify)
4. What is the monthly income of your family?
   ☐ Less than 2,000 yuan ☐ 2,000 yuan – 3,000 yuan
   ☐ 3,000 yuan – 4,000 yuan ☐ More than 4,000 yuan
5. What is the proposed amount of your monthly expenditure?
   ☐ Less than 300 yuan ☐ About 300 yuan to 400 yuan
   ☐ About 400 yuan to 500 yuan ☐ More than 500 yuan
6. What does your monthly expenditure mostly cover?
   ☐ Board and lodging ☐ Clothes
   ☐ Shopping ☐ Books and recreation
7. Do you think your expenditure is well arranged?
   ☐ Yes ☐ No ☐ Don't know
8. Do you make a monthly budget?
   ☐ Yes ☐ No
9. Do you take a part-time job?
   ☐ Yes (please specify) ☐ No
10. Do you borrow money from your classmates?
    ☐ Yes, often ☐ Yes, but seldom ☐ No
11. Do you often organize or attend parties?
    ☐ Yes ☐ No
12. Are you in love?
    ☐ Yes ☐ No
13. Are you a smoker or a drinker?
    ☐ Yes ☐ No
14. What do you think should be the acceptable amount of monthly expenditure for a college student?
    ☐ About 500 yuan ☐ between 500 yuan and 800 yuan
    ☐ More than 800 yuan

Sample 16 (6)

Railway Service Questionnaire

1. Is the train your most preferred mode of transport?
   ☐ Yes ☐ No (If no, please specify your most preferred mode)

2. How often do you travel by train?
   ☐ Once a week ☐ Once a month ☐ Occasionally ☐ Hard to say
3. The reason why you like to travel by train is
   ☐ It is more convenient   ☐ It is less expensive
   ☐ It saves time   ☐ Not sure
4. Are you satisfied with the punctuality of arrival and departure of the train in China?
   ☐ Yes   ☐ No
5. As a passenger, do you think you are well attended to?
   ☐ Yes   ☐ No
6. What do you think of CRH which has been just put into service?
   ☐ Excellent   ☐ Good in a general way
   ☐ No idea
7. Do you think the current price of a train ticket is acceptable and reasonable?
   ☐ Yes   ☐ No   ☐ Hard to say
8. What is your general impression of the railway service in China?
   ☐ Excellent   ☐ Good   ☐ Poor
   ☐ There is still room for improvement (please specify)
9. Have you ever filed a complaint about the service?
   ☐ Yes (please specify)   ☐ No
10. What are your suggestions to the railway authorities to further improve their service?
    _____
    _____

Sample 16 (7)

Questionnaire on Medical Care in Your City

1. I am in my
   ☐ Twenties   ☐ Thirties   ☐ Forties
   ☐ Fifties   ☐ Sixties and over
2. If you suffer from a minor illness, you will see a doctor in a(n)
   ☐ Ordinary clinic ☐ Community clinic
   ☐ Big hospital
3. How often do you have a regular physical check?
   ☐ Once a year ☐ Once every two years
   ☐ Never
4. Do you think doctors are reliable and trustworthy?
   ☐ Yes   ☐ No   ☐ Hard to say
5. Do you think doctors are patient enough when you describe the symptoms of your disease?
   ☐ Yes   ☐ No   ☐ Some doctors are, but some are not
6. Do you think an appointment is necessary before you go to see a doctor?
   ☐ Yes   ☐ No
   ☐ I never make an appointment with doctors
7. What do you think of the prices of medicines prescribed for you?
   ☐ Unbearably high ☐ Very high ☐ Acceptable and reasonable

8. Can your family cover the yearly medical expenses?
   ☐Yes   ☐No   ☐Almost yes   ☐Nearly no
9. Who do you think should shoulder the responsibility to cut down the high medical prices?
   ☐Government at all levels   ☐Hospitals
   ☐Pharmaceutical companies or factories
10. Do you think doctors should be paid a higher salary?
    ☐Yes   ☐No, they are well paid now
    ☐No idea
11. Have you ever filed a complaint to hospital authorities for any kinds of improper treatment rendered to you?
    ☐Yes   ☐No
12. Do you think the entry of foreign-funded hospitals into China poses some challenges to domestic hospitals?
    ☐Yes   ☐No   ☐Hard to say now
13. What are your suggestions on how to further improve the overall medical service in your city?
    _____

Sample 16（8）

Tourism Project Questionnaire

1. To which place or city have you traveled recently?
   ☐A scenic spot   ☐A neighboring city
   ☐A mountainous area   ☐A camping site
   ☐Other places of interest
2. Your modes of transport
   ☐Car   ☐Coach   ☐Train
   ☐Air   ☐Others（please specify）
3. Length of your stay
   ☐Less than five days   ☐A week
   ☐More than a week
4. Your accommodation
   ☐Hotel   ☐A camping site   ☐At my friend's   ☐Others
5. What are the major reasons for your visit?
   ☐Sightseeing   ☐Shopping
   ☐Recreation   ☐For an educational purpose
6. How much did the tour cost you?
   ☐Less than 1,000 yuan
   ☐Between 1,000 and 1,500 yuan
   ☐About 2,000 yuan
   ☐More than 2,000 yuan
7. Were you on a package tour?
   ☐Yes   ☐No

Unit 16 Questionnaires

8. If you were on a package tour, do you think you were well served?
   ☐ Yes (please be specific)   ☐ No (please be specific)
9. Will you recommend this scenic spot, place of interest, camping site to your friends?
   ☐ Yes   ☐ No
10. Will you visit the place for a second time?
    ☐ Yes   ☐ No   ☐ Don't know
11. Your suggestions:
    _____

16.4 NOTES

（1）Gallup poll　（美国）盖洛普民意测验
（2）a domestic brand　国内品牌
（3）deluxe　豪华的
（4）durable　耐用的
（5）after-sale service　售后服务
（6）outlets　折扣品经销店（奥特莱斯）
（7）rate　评价；划分等级
（8）prompt　快捷的
（9）campus activities　校园活动
（10）extra-curricular　课外的
（11）spoil　影响；损坏
（12）justify　为……辩护
（13）foster　培养
（14）committed　承担义务的；坚定的
（15）student-centered　以学生为中心的
（16）multi-media resources　多媒体资源
（17）bilingual teaching　双语教学
（18）put into service　投入运行；交付使用
（19）file a complaint　投诉
（20）prescribe　开……处方；规定
（21）pharmaceutical companies　制药公司
（22）coach　长途汽车
（23）a package tour　组团旅游；跟团旅游；包价旅游

16.5 COMMUNICATION LABORATORY

A. Give a brief answer to the following questions.
　　（1）What are questionnaires for?

(2) What factors must be taken into account when a questionnaire is designed?

(3) What goals are supposed to be reached after a questionnaire is conducted?

(4) What kind of writing style do you think should be adopted in designing a questionnaire?

B. Case Study

(1) You are working with the marketing department of Skyline Import and Export Corporation. Your manager asks you to design a questionnaire for overseas customers on the quality and after-sale service of a Chinese make air-conditioner. The questionnaire should include:

- When and where the air-conditioner was purchased;
- The user's general impression of the product, i. e. its price, appearance, color, etc;
- The quality of the purchased product;
- The after-sale service of the product.

After the questionnaire is conducted, try to analyze the data and information you have collected and write a report to your manager.

(2) Read the following passage and write a summary with about 200 words.

Most problems with questionnaire analysis can be traced back to the design phase of the project. Well-defined goals are the best way to assure a good questionnaire design. When the goals of a study can be expressed in a few clear and concise sentences, the design of the questionnaire becomes considerably easier. The questionnaire is developed to directly address the goals of the study.

One of the best ways to clarify your study goals is to decide how you intend to use the information. Do this before you begin designing the study. This sounds obvious, but many researchers neglect this task. Why do research if the results will not be used?

Be sure to commit the study goals to writing. Whenever you are unsure of a question, refer to the study goals and a solution will become clear. Ask only questions that directly address the study goals. Avoid the temptation to ask questions because it would be "interesting to know".

As a general rule, with only a few exceptions, long questionnaires get less response than short questionnaires. Keep your questionnaire short. In fact, the shorter the better. Response rate is the single most important indicator of how much confidence you can place in the results. A low response rate can be devastating to a study. Therefore, you must do everything possible to maximize the response rate. One of the most effective methods of maximizing response is to shorten the questionnaire.

If your survey is over a few pages, try to eliminate questions. Many people have difficulty knowing which questions could be eliminated. For the elimination round, read each question and ask, "How am I going to use this information?" If the information will be used in a decision-making process, then keep the question … it's important. If not, throw it out.

One important way to assure a successful survey is to include other experts and relevant decision-makers in the questionnaire design process. Their suggestions will improve the questionnaire and they will subsequently have more confidence in the results.

Formulate a plan for doing the statistical analysis during the design stage of the project. Know how every question will be analyzed and be prepared to handle missing data. If you cannot specify how you intend to analyze a question or use the information, do not use it in the survey.

Make the envelope unique. We all know how important first impressions are. The same holds true for questionnaires. The respondent's first impression of the study usually comes from the envelope containing the survey. The best envelopes (i.e., the ones that make you want to see what's inside) are colored, hand-addressed and use a commemorative postage stamp. Envelopes with bulk mail permits or gummed labels are perceived as unimportant. This will generally be reflected in a lower response rate.

Provide a well-written cover letter. The respondent's next impression comes from the cover letter. The importance of the cover letter should not be underestimated. It provides your best chance to persuade the respondent to complete the survey.

Give your questionnaire a title that is short and meaningful to the respondent. A questionnaire with a title is generally perceived to be more credible than one without it.

Include clear and concise instructions on how to complete the questionnaire. These must be very easy to understand, so use short sentences and basic vocabulary. Be sure to print the return address on the questionnaire itself (since questionnaires often get separated from the reply envelopes).

Begin with a few non-threatening and interesting items. If the first items are too threatening or "boring", there is little chance that the person will complete the questionnaire. People generally look at the first few questions before deciding whether or not to complete the questionnaire. Make them want to continue by putting interesting questions first.

Use simple and direct language. The questions must be clearly understood by the respondent. The wording of a question should be simple and to the point. Do not use uncommon words or long sentences. Make items as brief as possible. This will reduce misunderstandings and make the questionnaire appear easier to complete. One way to eliminate misunderstandings is to emphasize crucial words in each item by using bold, italics or underlining.

Leave adequate space for respondents to make comments. One criticism of questionnaires is their inability to retain the "flavor" of a response. Leaving space for comments will provide valuable information not captured by the response categories. Leaving white space also makes the questionnaire look easier and this increases response.

Place the most important items in the first half of the questionnaire. Respondents often send back partially completed questionnaires. By putting the most important items near the beginning, the partially completed questionnaires will still contain important information.

Hold the respondent's interest. We want the respondent to complete our questionnaire. One way to keep a questionnaire interesting is to provide variety in the type of items used. Varying the questioning format will also prevent respondents from falling into "response sets". At the same time, it is important to group items into coherent categories. All items should flow smoothly from one to the next.

If a questionnaire is more than a few pages and is held together by a staple, include some identifying data on each page (such as a respondent ID number). Pages often accidentally separate.

Provide incentives as a motivation for a properly completed questionnaire. What does the respondent get for completing your questionnaire? Altruism is rarely an effective motivator. Attaching a dollar bill to the questionnaire works well. If the information you are collecting is of interest to the respondent, offering a free summary report is also an excellent motivator. Whatever you choose, it must make the respondent want to complete the questionnaire.

Use professional production methods for the questionnaire—either desktop publishing or typesetting and keylining. Be creative. Try different colored inks and paper. The object is to make your questionnaire stand out from all the others the respondent receives.

Make it convenient. The easier it is for the respondent to complete the questionnaire the better. Always include a self-addressed postage-paid envelope. Envelopes with postage stamps get better response than business reply envelopes (although they are more expensive since you also pay for the non-respondents).

The final test of a questionnaire is to try it on representatives of the target audience. If there are problems with the questionnaire, they almost always show up here. If possible, be present while a respondent is completing the questionnaire and tell her that it is okay to ask you for clarification of any item. The questions she asks are indicative of problems in the questionnaire (i.e., the questions on the questionnaire must be without any ambiguity because there will be no chance to clarify a question when the survey is mailed).

References

Ansell, G. *English in Business: A Guide to Effective Business Writing* [M]. London: Pan Macmillan, 1985.

Bailey Jr., P. & Bailey, L. *The Plain English Approach to Business Writing* [M]. Oxford: Oxford University Press, 1997.

Doherty, M. *Writing for Business: Skills for Effective Report Writing in English* [M]. New York: Pearson English Language Teaching, 1987.

Dumaine, D. *Vest-Pocket Guide to Business Writing* [M]. Englewood Cliffs: Prentice Hall, 1996.

Emerson, F. B. *Technical Writing* [M]. Boston: Houghton Mifflin Company, 1987.

Ettinger, B. & Perfetto, L. E. *Business English: Writing in the Workplace* [M]. 4th ed. Englewood Cliffs: Prentice Hall, 2006.

Geffner, B. A. *Business English* [M]. 4th ed. New York: Barron's Educational Series, 2003.

Gerson, S. J. & Steven, M. G. *Technical Writing: Process and Product* [M]. Beijing: Higher Education Press, 2004.

Halpern, J. W., Judith, M. K. & Agnes, L. *Business Writing Strategies and Samples* [M]. New York: Macmillan, 1988.

Hatch, R. A. *Business Writing* [M]. Chicago: Science Research Associates Inc., 1983.

Luthans, F. & Doh, J. *International Management: Culture, Strategy, and Behavior* [M]. 10th ed. New York: McGraw-Hill Education, 2018.

Piotrowski, M. *Effective Business Writing* (2nd edition) [M]. New York: Harper Collins Publishers, 1996.

Stewart, M. M., et al. *Business English and Communication* [M]. New York: McGraw-Hill Inc., 1978.

Wilson, M. *Writing for Business* [M]. Nashville: Thomas Nelson & Sons Ltd., 1988.

边毅, 肖曼君, 曾涛. 商务英语写作[M]. 北京: 清华大学出版社, 2003.

常玉田. 英语商务报告写作[M]. 北京: 外文出版社, 2004.

胡英坤. 实用商务英语写作[M]. 大连: 大连理工大学出版社, 2000.

李小飞. 商务英语专题写作[M]. 北京: 中国商务出版社, 2004.

陆乃圣. 最新英语应用文大全[M]. 北京: 世界图书出版公司, 2002.

石定乐, 蔡蔚. 实用商务英语写作[M]. 北京: 北京理工大学出版社, 2003.

王光林. 商务英语应用文大全[M]. 北京: 东方出版中心, 1998.